Feng Shui
So Easy a Child Can Do It

Pat Heydlauff

Feng Shui, So Easy a Child Can Do It
Copyright © 2023 by Pat Heydlauff, All Rights Reserved
ISBN: 978-0-9983347-7-6

ALL RIGHTS RESERVED. This book contains material protected under International and Federal Copyright Laws and Treaties. Any unauthorized reprint or use of this material is prohibited. No part of this book may be reproduced or transmitted in any form or by any means, electronic or mechanical, including photocopying, recording, or by any information storage and retrieval system without express written permission from the author / publisher.

Edited by Dawn Josephson
Cover Design by Janet Aiossa

First Edition, Published by Jasmine-Jade Enterprises, LLC, 2008

Second Edition, Published by Createspace, 2011

Third Edition, Published by Energy Design, 2023

Feng Shui
So Easy a Child Can Do It

Dedication

To those who wish to take control of their lives so they can create a better tomorrow.

Contents

Author's Note 11
Chapter 1: Demystifying Feng Shui 15
   An Ancient Concept for a 21st Century Way of Life.........15
   Energy to Support You..16
   Will Feng Shui Work for You?..30
Chapter 2: The Shape of Life 31
   Can Using Feng Shui Be That Easy? 31
   The Variety of Schools..32
   Best Directions and Numbers..38
   My Preference 39
   Summary 43
Chapter 3: First Stop – Outside Your Front Door 45
   Energize Your Front Yard First..47
   Create Outdoor Retreats 51
   Design Patios for Downtime...53
   Winter Retreat Plans 56
   Enjoy Positive Outdoor Energy All Year Long.................56
Chapter 4: Next Stop – Inside Your Front Door..................59
   Energy Needs to Meander Throughout.............................59
   Overcoming Structural Flaws 60
   Home Décor Can Prevent Energy Movement 63
   Is the Energy Still Stuck?..65
   Color, Shape, and Sound..67

Chapter 5: Calm Your Chaos 79
   Chaos Creates Negative Energy.............................. 80
   Calm Your Chaos with a Plan................................ 81
   The Bedroom 82
   The Kitchen... 86
   Complete Your Calming Plan................................ 91
   Create a Sanctuary for Peace................................ 93
   Positive Energy Provides Desired Results 95

Chapter 6: Do You Have the Relationship You Want? 97
   Life Is All about Relationships 98
   Define Your Relationships.................................... 99
   What Type of Relationship Do You Want with Yourself? 100
   What Kind of Personal Relationships Do You Want with Others? 103
   Create Balanced Relationship Energy 109

Chapter 7: A New You – Imagine It Now! 111
   It's All about You... 112
   Reflect So You Can Unclutter............................. 115
   Feng Shui Your Thinking.................................... 118
   Storing Positive Energy 119
   Create an Intentions Board to Accomplish Goals 122
   Create Your Best Life Now 125

Chapter 8: What You Wear Matters 127
   Does Your Wardrobe Support You? 128
   An Energized Wardrobe Energizes You 130
   Begin with Your Existing Wardrobe................... 132

Create Energy to Match Your Day *133*
The Right Energy for the Job *136*
Shop with Energy in Mind *138*
Energized Wardrobes Really Work *139*

Chapter 9: If Your Child's Wall Could Talk 141

Does Feng Shui Work for Children Too? *142*
Color Energy Makes a Difference *142*
Peaceful Color Palette for Children *144*
Infants and Preschoolers *145*
The School-Aged Child *146*
The Teen Years *149*
Unclutter to Promote Creativity *150*
Positive Energy Brings Desired Results *152*

Chapter 10: From Clutter and Stress to Workplace Success 153

Reduce Stress—Improve Success *154*
Increase Prosperity by Aligning Thoughts, Actions, and Surroundings *155*
Define Success to Increase Clarity *163*
Feng Shui Can Help You on Your Journey to Success .. *164*

Chapter 11: How to Thrive—Not Just Survive—the Holidays 167

Enjoy the Holidays More *168*
Create Positive Energy by Being Thankful *170*
Energize Now to Ensure a Joyful Holiday Season *173*
Unclutter First *173*
Energize Next *174*

Listen *174*
Feel *175*
Taste *175*
Smell *175*
See *175*
Holiday Stress-Reducing Guide *176*
New Year's Resolutions That Matter *177*
Thrive on Holiday Energy—All Year Long *179*
Chapter 12: Conclusion – Stepping Stones 181
Recipe for Positive Thinking *182*
Positive Thinking = Positive Results *182*
Positive Energy Shifts = Positive Thinking *183*
What Does Your "Balance" Look Like? *185*
Your Personal Roadmap *188*
Does Feng Shui Really Matter? *188*
Is Positive Change on Your Calendar? *190*
The Result *190*
Resources 193
About the Author 195

Author's Note

When I wrote the first edition of *Feng Shui So Easy a Child Can Do It* in 2008, the world had just welcomed in the new millennium and "Y2K" was everywhere. While the banks, businesses, computers, and world clocks did not come crashing down, my life did. I had parted ways years earlier with a stressful, energy-draining career filled with high anxiety, excessive travel, and constant stress—all of which took a toll on my physical and spiritual well-being.

At the time, I did not know how to control the stress, eliminate negative thinking, and create the balanced world my body and mind were desperately seeking. I was drowning in old thinking and all sorts of clutter in my surroundings and mind, with no visible way out, much like the world we live in today.

Then, just when I thought things couldn't get any worse, an accident (of my own creation) left me temporarily blind in my right eye. Not only had the lens in my eye been shattered, so had my life.

Looking back, I see so many parallels between my life back then and what is currently happening in society. In 2020, COVID dealt humanity a major blow physically, emotionally, and spiritually. We were further assaulted with job loss, businesses closing, inflation, interest rates rising, and talk of government corruption here and abroad.

As a result, the high anxiety stressors people experience has dramatically increased in our post-COVID, high inflation, fear-based, chaotic world—a world that requires calm and quiet to heal and create anew. But calm and quiet are nowhere to be found.

So how do we change this? The same way I changed my life decades ago. I allowed my creative right-brain side to take control of my life because I needed balance, quiet, and peace more than ever. This began a long journey inward that at times seemed endless, like a vast wilderness with no roadmap, no instruction manual, and no way home. Somewhere in the middle of my searching I started down a pathway called Feng Shui. It was drawing me in like a magnet, pulling me closer and closer to the mysteries of hope, peace, and joy held by an ancient Chinese civilization.

Some aspects of this journey nurtured my soul and supported my personal belief systems, while others challenged it. At the same time, I expanded my creativity to incorporate fine art painting and writing daily in my journal. These activities created balance in my world and I became increasingly spiritual in nature. My Inner Spirit was being nurtured. Through this creativity, my life became more "balanced" and feelings of harmony were gradually taking the place of anxiety and stress. The Feng Shui lifestyle I adopted provided me a peace-filled sanctuary necessary to thrive. I discovered that my life was filled with clutter (physical and mental) that no longer worked for me and did not provide me supportive positive energy. So I began my physical and mental decluttering process.

While on my personal journey, I read through thousands of pages of books and manuscripts and listened to Feng Shui masters in person and electronically, searching for that magic bullet to make everything better. Finally, I figured it out! What

I needed was to distill the relevant knowledge from all the information I had processed, to synthesize it down into something that was easy to understand and even easier to use. So that's exactly what I did when I wrote this book years ago.

In this new edition, I've updated the information to make it even more relevant for the realities we face in this new world of increased chaos and turmoil.

As a result of my long pilgrimage years ago, I am continually eliminating the stressors in my life, creating calm quiet space around me, and achieving balance and peace without and within. I am living a life filled with nurturing supportive positive energy all day long…a life where I am in control. You can experience the same!

Living a stress-free, peace-filled lifestyle based on Feng Shui principles is even more relevant now than when I wrote the first edition of this book. Today, the world is bombarded with much greater levels of stress, anxiety, and chaos than before. Thanks to social media and 24/7 news cycles that we can't escape, we are all reacting to fear-driven forces that are deliberately separating society into groups and pitting them against each other. As a result, we need to find or create chaos-free quiet sanctuaries in our homes so we can hear our spiritual voice within where truth, peace, and joy reside. Feng Shui is a roadmap to finding exactly that.

This book is a direct result of my journey. In some ways, it is part of my journey, or at least how I discovered for the first time that I could control my own life and create my present and future through positive energy. This book brings to you, the reader, a unique perspective to achieving balance and decreasing stress. It will help you enrich your life, your home, or your office, creating environments with balance, harmony, and a positive flow of energy.

As you digest the information on these pages, you will find your soul feeling nurtured. Feng Shui is not only about your physical environment; it is also about your thinking and bringing it into alignment with your surroundings, your life goals, and the spiritual aspects of your life. That is the true path to achieving your hopes, dreams, peace, and joy.

While this book is designed for reading, it is also a functional manual you can use as a reference book to help you create a better, more productive, and more abundant life.

May this book help you realize your hopes and dreams so you can create your own piece of heaven on earth.

Joy and peace within,
Pat Heydlauff

Chapter 1

Demystifying Feng Shui

An Ancient Concept for a 21st Century Way of Life

Feng Shui is an ancient Chinese philosophy I've adapted for use in the twenty-first century. It works better today than it did 3,000 years ago, as it provides you with a positive way to deal with twenty-first-century stressors and enables you to create peace-filled sanctuaries in your home and workplace. In today's chaotic, instant-messaging, frantic world, people are searching for hope, peace, joy, progress, and positive change. As a result, the principles of Feng Shui have more relevance now than ever before.

A modern-day name for Feng Shui could be *Energy Cultivation*—the use of positive energy in your personal environment to create calm and balance in your life, while still honoring *your* existing beliefs, such as your personal religious convictions.

For example, instead of a Buddha or Fu dogs, Christian families might place symbols of their religious faith throughout their homes, such as crosses or pictures and statues of Mary, Jesus, the Archangels, and numerous saints. These symbols are meaningful to their life, provide a source of positive energy or emotional comfort, and serve as the foundation for the family's values and respect for others.

Similarly, Jewish families may have a collection of menorahs in their homes and a *mezuah* on the front doorpost to bless those entering their home. They may have additional *mezuzot* on other doors to bless their coming and going from those rooms as well. Again, these symbols, along with those observed by other religions, become part of the energizing process for these families in their homes.

Feng Shui supports the creation of positive energy by being inclusive of the existing beliefs, faith, and principles already established in a home.

Energy to Support You

People often ask me, "What, exactly, is Feng Shui?" In order to dispel any misunderstandings or myths, I often answer by telling people what Feng Shui is *not*. It is definitely not a religion, a cult, some type of magic, or a bandage for fixing your life. Feng Shui is a way of life you choose in order to create balance and harmony in your personal environment so that you can bring about a better and more enjoyable future.

My simple definition of Feng Shui is the use of positive energy to bring about desired results, such as better health, more income, and abundance in all areas of life. The ancient Chinese studied and used Feng Shui every day to survive and to enhance well-being, longevity, and prosperity.

At this point you might ask, "What does energy have to do with Feng Shui?"

The answer is everything. The literal translation of Feng Shui is "wind and water," two of the dominant energy forces on Earth. Our bodies, our planet, and our solar system are all related to each other and "glued" together with energy.

Energy from many sources makes our world go around. The sun's energy gives us warmth and light. The wind's energy gives us cool breezes and, when harnessed, can become a source for electricity. Gravitational energy keeps people grounded and prevents us from floating into outer space.

Our world is made up of energy. The north and south poles have magnetic energy, which is found when using a compass. We have an east–west movement of energy as the earth rotates on its axis. Other examples include heat energy from fire, cool energy from water, growing energy in trees and soil, and energy that results when molten metal cools and is formed into tools, equipment, and automobiles. Feng Shui energy is simply a way of harnessing some of that wonderful universe-energy and putting it to good use in our personal lives.

We all have personal energy as well. When you surround yourself with positive people, uplifting ideas, and things that please you, you feel good about yourself because all these positive things and people give you good energy. If you live in a dark home, surround yourself with negative people, and focus on pessimistic thinking, you will likely find yourself depressed, discouraged, and not feeling well because of the negative energy. A simple rule to remember is:

Positive energy contributes to your well-being.

Feng Shui utilizes positive energy to support you and your beliefs, revitalize the soul, unclutter the home, and eliminate negative self-talk. By using various basic Feng Shui principles, you can be more productive and fulfilled, both at home and in the workplace.

Perhaps the biggest benefit of Feng Shui is the uncluttering of both your physical and emotional worlds to allow positive energy to enter. An important aspect of uncluttering is that it helps you balance your surroundings, or personal environment. The placement of household objects and art can provide additional balance and energize areas of your life that seem to be stuck.

You can transform your home into a peaceful refuge from the frantic world outside and make it a place where you can find your balance again—a place that flows with positive energy. When your home feels peaceful, your mind and body do as well. Likewise, you can transform your workplace into a space that enables you to focus better and be more productive. When your workplace is filled with positive energy, you will experience planned, intentional success.

The results? You're a calmer, more focused, and more productive person. You get more pleasure out of life. You're better able to determine which things to keep and which to throw out…not only from your closet but also from your life. Your home becomes a place of peace and harmony and a true refuge from the everyday pressures of the outside world. Your workspace becomes a place where preparation and opportunity meet.

Through this process, you'll learn to determine what you can control and what you cannot. You'll be better able to live in the now instead of worrying about past events or possible future events that may never happen. You will, basically, create your own personal roadmap to living your life to the fullest.

The choice is quite simple. If you want to feel well, have a bright outlook on life, and find peace and happiness within, surround yourself with things you love and people who provide you with great energy. Feng Shui is your tool for doing precisely that. To help you get started, I've divided some very basic Feng Shui principles into three options that you can use individually or at the same time.

Option 1: Calm Your Surroundings

You can use Feng Shui principles to create positive energy in your personal surroundings and home and to begin a general balancing process. These principles universally apply to everyone and will provide the same general results—balancing and creating harmony.

- Unclutter every room, closet, and cupboard in your house and garage. Clutter can be anything from stacks of magazines and "stuff" you've collected over the years to clothing that no longer fits and Aunt Suzie's dishes you've never liked. *Get rid of them!*
- Do not replace the removed clutter with new stuff! Energy needs to meander slowly throughout your home and loves to find cleared open spaces in which to rest. That's how new ideas, better health, and a better life begin—with new energy that lingers.
- Place your bed as far away from the entrance door to your bedroom as possible. But make sure your feet don't point out the door. This provides maximum positive energy and safety.
- Do not store things under your bed. This ensures that when you sleep, energy can completely circulate around

your body, providing you optimal rest. This will allow you to wake up refreshed and re-energized.
- Paint your bedroom walls soft, soothing colors conducive to rest. Low-energy pastels are perfect bedroom energy.
- Leave all internal doors open throughout your home, whether a room is regularly used or not. Each room fulfills an energy sector within your house; therefore, it is important that energy passes through those areas even though they may not be used every day.
- Paint living room and kitchen walls slightly more energetic colors to encourage good nourishment of the body and mind. The slightly raised energetic value provides improved nutrition and positive interaction with family members.
- Prevent energy that enters your front door from shooting right through your home and out a window or door directly opposite it by using furniture or rug runners to re-direct the energy into other parts of the house. (If you can't redirect the energy with physical objects, hang a thirty-millimeter, round, multifaceted crystal from the ceiling inside your front door.)
- Create a "quiet zone" in your home in a spare bedroom, basement, or loft so that various members of the family can find a place of peace when they need to retreat from the cares and worries of the day. Spend at least fifteen minutes, three times a week, in the "quiet zone" and ask others not to disturb you. We are a society bombarded with noise pollution and this is your escape.
- Locate the southeast wealth area of your home or living room and energize it with a money plant, good-luck indoor bamboo plant, or a large upward-reaching plant. Keep this plant healthy. The moment it looks unhealthy, toss it and replace it immediately.

- Energize the southwest relationship area of your home with pictures of you and your family or friends having a great time together. This also works with business associates, improving work relationships.
- Place a bowl of fruit on your kitchen table or kitchen counter to energize abundance. (Yes, you can use good-looking, colorful faux fruit if you cannot possibly eat the fresh fruit before it would spoil.)
- Energize the north career/spiritual area of your home by placing a small water fountain there. You can also hang a picture of a gently flowing stream or use the colors deep blue and/or purple in that area. This works well for those searching for a new career, wanting improvement in their current career, or searching spiritually for peace within.
- Be sure to keep all toilet seat lids and as many drains as possible closed to prevent energy from literally running down the drain.

Balance is about:
What you surround yourself with
Who you surround yourself with
Choices you make in your daily life
What you do to yourself physically
What you do to yourself mentally

It is a learned trait that provides peace and harmony through your surroundings and provides peace within.

Option 2: Create Harmony Using Yin and Yang

People often ask me, "Do Yin and Yang have anything to do with Feng Shui?" Yes, Yin and Yang have *everything* to do with Feng Shui. They are used in all philosophies and schools of Feng Shui.

Yin and Yang represent perfect balance. For example, weather that is not too hot nor too cold could be described as perfect Yin and Yang. Another example would be a room that has the right proportions of dark and light furnishings to make you feel comfortable. Think of Yin and Yang as that equal energy near the middle that provides the best positive energy, personal balance, peace, and harmony. Yang is considered strong energy from the heavens or the universe, and Yin is considered a softer energy from the earth. Yin/Yang balance is the underpinning for our planet.

You can use Yin and Yang to describe all direct opposites. For example, activities such as reading a book, sitting on the beach, or listening to peaceful music are very passive and Yin. But activities such as swimming, playing tennis, or bicycling are very active and are Yang. If you overdo on the first you can become lethargic. If you overdo on the second you can become overly stimulated. Balance is found somewhere in the middle.

When it comes to home furnishings, those pieces that are soft, curvy, or supple with warmer colors or flowing lines are Yin. Those with hard edges, tight upholstery, or reflective surfaces with cooler colors or sharp angles are Yang. For example, if you have light-colored tile on your floors, that is very Yang and needs to be balanced with Yin furniture or decorative accessories in warmer colors and softer fabrics. If the walls in your rooms are dark, they are very Yin and need to be balanced with lighter-colored furnishing.

Too much Yang in a room may be exciting at first, but eventually it can create aggressive and angry thinking and feelings. Too much Yin in a room might at first seem peaceful, but eventually it could lead to passive and even depressing feelings and thinking.

You can also apply this thought process to clothing. If you have a Yang personality (high-energy Type A) and you want to become more Yin, try softening your clothing by wearing garments that are soft to the touch, are deeper in value, are warmer colors, and drape or flow in the wind. If your personality is more Yin and you wish to strengthen your demeanor and become more Yang, wear clothing that's sharp, crisp, light-colored, and is fitted or more structured in nature.

Using the principles of Yin and Yang goes a long way toward creating harmony in your home and in your personal life. And no one will ever know you are using some Feng Shui techniques to do it.

Yin can be described as:

- Cooler, slower, darker, gentler, paler, softer, and more passive
- Thin wavy lines, horizontal rectangles, and broad oval shapes
- Matte or textured surfaces, natural wood, and fabrics
- Black, gold, and purple
- Female

Yang can be described as:

- Hotter, faster, stronger, brighter, lighter, more active, and aggressive
- Circular, octagonal, square, and angular in shape
- Hard, shiny, reflective surfaces, glass, polished marble, and stainless steel
- White, blue, silver
- Male

This is the universally recognized symbol for Yin and Yang. Notice that there always is a balance of dark in the light and light in the dark.

Using a balance of Yin/Yang that meets your energy needs is one of the simplest ways to use

Feng Shui in your home and create harmony. By evaluating each room in your home based upon a few of the characteristics mentioned previously, you can create a wonderful, harmonious sense of well-being.

If you dislike going into one room because you are never comfortable there, look closely at it and determine if it is too light or too dark. If too dark, lighten it up with torchiere lamps, bright throw pillows, or light-colored artwork and pull open the curtains. If too light, tone it down with darker throw rugs or lap robes and dim the lights. You achieve balance by placing some dark in the light or some light in the dark.

Option 3: Create Balance with the Five Elements

Another of the foundations of Feng Shui energy used by all philosophies and schools is the use of the five elements: water, wood, fire, earth, and metal. You can dramatically improve balance in your environment and your personal well-being by simply harnessing and using these specific natural energies that Mother Nature provides.

The proper use of the elements is another easy way to create better energy in your home or office. The only rule to follow regarding this option is:

Use a balanced (not necessarily equal) amount of each element in every room.

Considering there are only five elements to deal with, this should be a relatively easy process. This rule, however, is a touch arbitrary because "a balanced amount" depends on your personality as well as where you live. Also, I will caution you, overdoing one or two of the elements in any given room can throw off the balance in that room and you will feel uncomfortable every time you enter it.

Following are some guidelines for using the five basic elements to create better energy and maintain balance in your world.

Water

The water element is represented by deep blues and purples or wavy lines in these colors. This element is best used in small quantities, such as tabletop water fountains, pictures with water (lakes, oceans, and rivers), or the actual colors. The water element is cooling, so it is great in a warm, south-facing room, but can be cold and unwelcoming in cooler north-facing rooms, especially if you paint the walls blue. Too much of this element can be depressing. If you need more of the water element in a room you can add some of the metal element. If your room has too much of the water element, you can create balance by using items from the fire and wood elements.

Wood

The wood element is represented by plants, trees, wooden items, the color green, and tall thin rectangular shapes. This is a health- and wealth-oriented element with a healing color and can be used more than most of the other elements. You can add the wood element easily to all rooms through wooden pieces of furniture, wood flooring, pictures of trees, plants (live or silk) of various sizes, along with green-colored items. If you need more of the wood element you can add some of the earth element. If there is too much wood in your office or home, balance it by using items from the metal and fire elements.

Fire

The fire element is best represented by the color red and items that reach upward and end with points on the top such as mountains, pyramids, and candles. Use this element sparingly as it can energize a room enough to create "heated arguments" and a hyper-nervous atmosphere. You can use splashes of the fire element in shades of red or upward pointed shapes to warm up a cool north-facing room or to energize a cozy earth-toned room. Ideally, use the fire element in accent pieces, such as pillows and artwork, rather than a large piece of furniture. Think about how you feel when you wear a red dress or a red necktie. Either will give you a personal energy boost. In general, do not use red in the dining or breakfast room, as it stimulates the appetite and is not conducive to quiet conversation. If a room has too much of the fire element, add some of the earth and water elements to tone it down and create balance.

Earth

The earth element is represented by soft flowing items like upholstered furniture, throws, flowing curtains, low rectangular shapes, all the earth tone colors, especially terra cotta, ceramics, glass, and those objects made of the earth. This is a peaceful and relaxing element that should take up a large percentage of space in rooms where you wish to relax, sleep, or be together with the family doing quiet things. However, if there is too much earth in any given room you can become lethargic and unmotivated. If you have a room that needs more earth energy you can add some of the fire element. If your room has too much of the wood element, add some of the wood and metal elements for balance.

Metal

The metal element is represented by the various metals, such as gold, silver, copper, brass, pewter, and so on. Those same colors, plus white and the round shape of a circle, also represent metal. This is a highly energizing element, great for offices or rooms where lots of activity takes place, such as the kitchen. In other areas, go lightly. To further energize the colors or shapes of the metal element, you can add more of the earth element. If your rooms have white walls, white furniture, and light-colored flooring, you may find it uncomfortable to sit and relax in such space. Add some of the fire and wood elements to bring it back into balance.

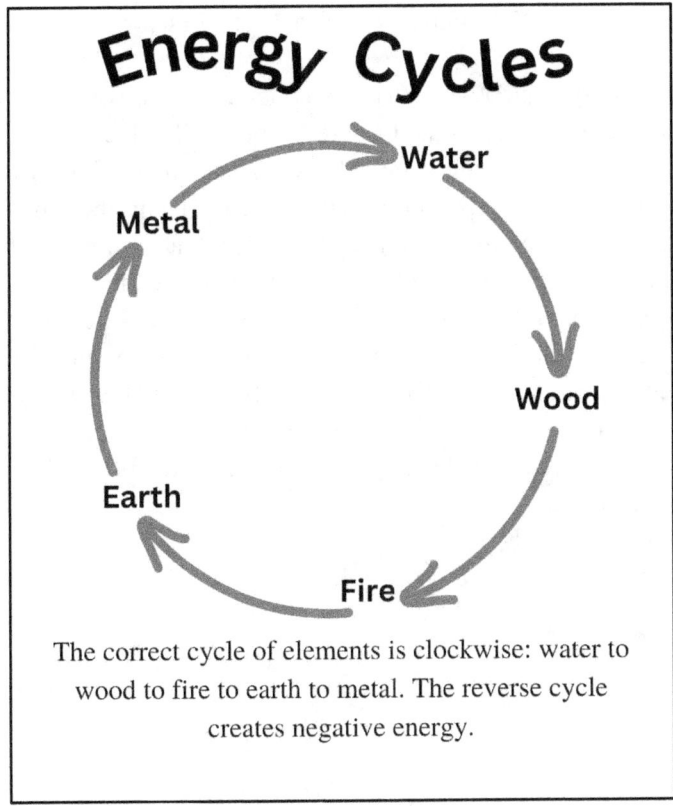

The correct cycle of elements is clockwise: water to wood to fire to earth to metal. The reverse cycle creates negative energy.

Creating balance using the elements is fun and easy. As mentioned earlier, factors such as your personality and where you live will impact how much of each element you need to create balance in your environment. In the United States, the average home contains approximately sixty-five percent of wood and earth elements, thirty percent of metal and water elements, and five percent of the fire element. Use these simple rules of balance in every room, including your office. They work every time and, just as with the Yin and Yang option, no one will know you used Feng Shui to do it.

Will Feng Shui Work for You?

Absolutely yes! Whether you use one or all three of the Feng Shui options presented here, you will feel definite improvements in your personal environment that will lead you to balance, harmony, and a better life. By using the tools in this section, along with the principles that follow in the coming chapters, you will have many resources that will help make a positive energy difference in your life. The specific things you implement will vary depending upon your energy needs, goals, and objectives. Ultimately you will discover that when your world is balanced, your health, wealth, and prosperity improve, leading to a better, more fulfilling, and abundant life.

Chapter 2

The Shape of Life

Can Using Feng Shui Be That Easy?

When I'm speaking to groups, people often tell me that Feng Shui appears to be confusing. They read one book and learn one approach, and then they read another book only to learn that it's in conflict with the first book. A third book might have yet another philosophy, adding to the confusion.

Even though they are interested in Feng Shui and would like to use its principles to improve their lives, they often give up because of the confusion and frustration. Invariably at this point in my presentation, several members of the audience are nodding their heads in agreement, acknowledging similar experiences.

The Variety of Schools

Feng Shui is a vast subject with lots to learn, but it doesn't have to be confusing or contradictory. There are different schools of teaching for this ancient art. The most common four schools of Feng Shui are the Form School, the Compass School, the Western School (sometimes referred to as the Black Hat Sect School), and the Flying Star School (also known as the 9 Ki School). There is also a version of Feng Shui not used as frequently in the United States, but practiced in India, called the Vaastu Shashtra.

All the schools are built around Ch'i (chee), the invisible life-force energy that surrounds and resides in all of us and all things. Ch'i is that great feeling of joy in your heart when you receive good news, such as the arrival of your first grandchild, or the feeling of overwhelming relief in the pit of your stomach, such as when the medical tests you were nervous about reveal that you are fine. Ch'i can also be that awful feeling you get in the pit of your stomach when the phone rings at 3:00 in the morning or how you feel when the hair on the back of your neck prickles as you hear an unexpected sound behind you.

Good Feng Shui requires Ch'i to flow and meander throughout your home, workplace, and life so it can help you create prosperity and abundance. If it flows too quickly or becomes stagnant, your energy becomes unbalanced and lost, or it gets stuck in various areas of your life. The objective is to create a personal environment that provides you supportive harmonious energy that enables you to not only survive, but also thrive.

Let's briefly review each school of thought.

The Form School

The original school of Feng Shui is 3,000-plus years old. The Form School focuses on the external landscape and the orientation of your property as it relates to its environment. It deals with the areas of shape and the movement of energy. The Form School first looks at the landscape's shape, form, and size in relationship to a home or office building. Then it looks at the movement of energy around buildings and through natural watercourses, as well as the avoidance of straight alignments of roads and structures, which create negative energy called poison arrows. The Form School uses direction plus animal symbolism to represent the various natural landscape forms. Following is a chart that outlines this school of Feng Shui.

East	The Green Dragon	Tall trees representing mid-sized hills to bring you material success, wealth, and power
South	The Phoenix Bird	A small hill or mound in front of your home for luck and opportunity
West	The White Tiger	Landscape that is lower than the east and slopes away from the home such as low shrubs to bring you protection
North	The Black Turtle	Large hills or mountains behind you to bring you steady improvement and prosperity

The Compass School

Many people consider The Compass School to be the traditional school. It is based on a formula using an octagon-shaped tool or map called a "Bagua," with each of the eight directions given a value, such as health, prosperity, relationship, career, etc. You use this tool by aligning its compass directions with the directions of your home and then placing it over your floor plan. The Bagua becomes a map to determine the flow of energy in various areas of your home or office. Based on your personal needs, the map will show you the areas you need to unclutter and enhance. In this school, north always represents career.

As you review the Bagua image below, notice that south is at the top of this map. The ancient Chinese considered south the most important direction, as it faces the nurturing warmth of the sun and is believed to bring good fortune. In the United States, north is usually placed at the top of a compass.

The number 5 is always found in the center of the Bagua and is regarded as an auspicious number. It has an implied meaning of harmony represented by the Yin and Yang symbol.

This map is also associated with a similar Feng Shui tool, with nine equal squares, three across and three down, without the compass directions, used by the Black Hat Sect School, which we'll explore next.

Bagua (also known as Pa Kua)
Eight Main Life Aspirations or Goals

The Black Hat Sect School

Founded in the United States in 1986, this form of Feng Shui is also known as the Black Hat Sect Tantric Buddhist School, or the Western School. In this school, rather than using the traditional compass directions and Bagua, it uses a Nine Life Areas map where each square contains a number that represents a certain life aspiration, goal, or objectives.

4 Wealth	9 Fame	2 Relationships
3 Family	5 Health	7 Children
8 Wisdom	1 Career	6 Helpful People

You'll notice that the Black Hat Sect school Bagua, or map, is identical in shape to the Lo Shu Square that follows and does not have any compass directions. The numbering system and symbolism as noted in the Compass School Bagua are the same in the Black Hat Sect School and the Flying Star School. They always align the career sector to the front door of the home or office building or to the side of the building with the front door if it is not centered. Each room is then evaluated from the position of the location of this door.

The Flying Star School

The Flying Star (or 9 Ki) School uses the information from the Bagua (used in the Compass School), including the compass directions and the elements, and adds another tool known as the Lo Shu Square or Lo Shu Diagram. While this is one of the more difficult schools to master, it takes into consideration many of the unseen influences in a person's life and business in addition to direction. It is often thought of as a form of Chinese astrology.

The Shape of Life

In this school, the user is assigned one of the nine numbers below based on their date of birth. Charts are available for determining this number (see the references at the back of the book). Every year, each number moves into the next higher numerical square until each number has passed through all nine squares and returns to its original square, where it begins another nine-year journey. For example, if your number is 1 the year you were born, the next year it will move to the square currently occupied by number 2, and the following year it will move to the square occupied by the number 3. Each square has significance for a person's life experiences, much like astrology. The square below is a beginning Lo Shu Square and represents the year 2000.

4	9	2
3	5	7
8	1	6

While many of the Feng Shui schools have common ground, such as the flow of positive energy, the five elements, removing clutter, and a Yin/Yang concept for balance, their differences can be staggering and confusing. As noted, compass directions matter, though not in the Black Hat Sect.

Also, most schools have a tool that serves as a map or a guide to help you determine where the various areas are in your home and how to effectively energize them.

Best Directions and Numbers

You do not need have neither your personal numbers nor best direction information to follow the easy-to-use information in this manual. It is important, however, that you know it is available.

People are often confused about the best and worst direction numbers. Many formulas exist to help you determine your personal best and worst directions, but there are also many variables. For example, a male and female born on the same day will have a different number. Were you were born between January 1 and February 20? If so, then you need to check the date on which the Chinese New Year fell the year of your birth. If your best number happens to be 5, you will be routed to a different number depending on whether you are male or female. Also, depending on the Feng Shui School of teaching, the formula used to determine your number will create a different number. For example, the number in the Lo Shui School will differ from the others.

Again, knowing your best directions and numbers isn't required. However, there is value in knowing that such information is available for future use. See the "Resources" section at the back of the book to find additional information on the Flying Star School that provides their formula or, better yet, a chart where the work has already been done. Simply look at the date when you were born and the information is right there.

My Preference

Since the early 1990s, I have studied the writings of many Feng Shui Masters. I've listened to live presentations from different schools. After much research and evaluation, I settled on the Compass School as my primary foundation of Feng Shui knowledge. Whether speaking, writing, or consulting, I also select relevant and necessary information from the Form School and the Flying Star School.

I chose the Compass School because, as the name suggests, it is based on the use of a compass and the energy representations of its eight primary directions. The principles of the Compass School most closely align with the naturally occurring energy fields on our planet with its significant magnetic energy fields at the north and south poles. In addition, the rotation of the Earth on its axis and its revolution around the sun result in other major east-west energy fields. To me, that placed even more value on the need to respect not only the natural energy flow on Earth, but also on the north-south and east-west directions in which those energy patterns travel. Since not all Feng Shui schools incorporate direction and the natural flow of Earth's energy, this became an important factor in my decision as to which school I preferred.

Each of the four primary directions—North, South, East and West—plus each of the four secondary directions—Northeast, Southeast, Southwest, and Northwest—takes on a special meaning or value in the Compass School. And there are specific methods of increasing the energy flow in each of these directions, depending on your needs and where you want energy focused on in your life.

For example, the sun rises in the East, bringing with it the birth of a new day, new growth, and new beginnings. Therefore, east is associated with the development of new things in your life, such as a new business, new friends, a new job, or new additions to your family or business. It also correlates to growth, improved health, and higher income. East is further energized by the wood element, and by using symbols of growth, such as plants and trees (the very essence of growth every new day), and the color green. Springtime, for example, would also be considered part of the direction east.

Each of the eight directions in Compass School Feng Shui is assigned appropriate values, often called the eight Life Aspirations or goals, elements, numbers, seasons of the year, and events. Using the compass directions makes it easy to understand the logic behind applying Feng Shui energy principles to improve your life. It also takes away much of the confusion created by the various schools of teaching.

A map can help you determine how the different areas of your home or office are impacted by the energy flowing through them, as well as which elements and colors would improve each area. I've created a simple tool called the Shape of Life Map, incorporating the best of all the previous tools.

The Shape of Life

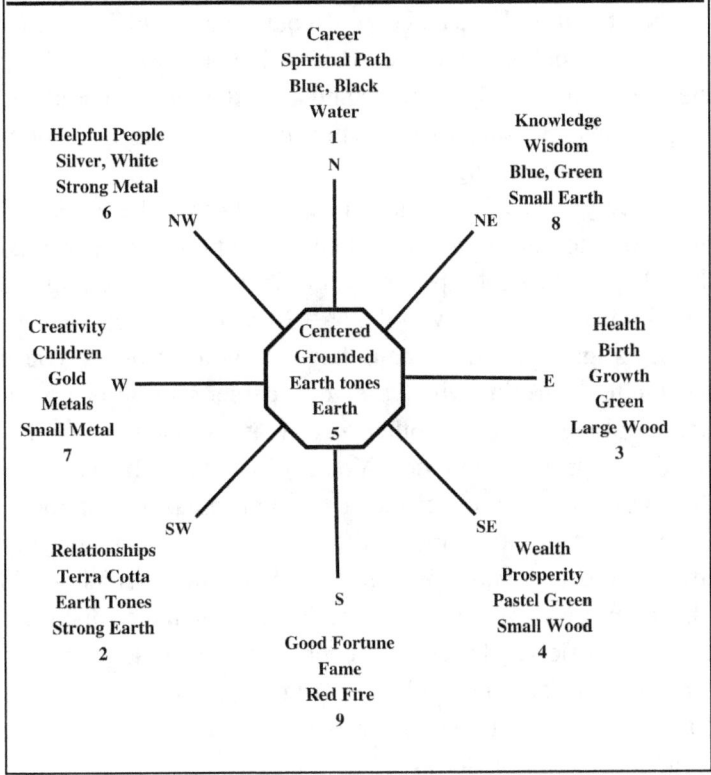

The Shape of Life Map is quite easy to use. All you need is a compass, which most cell phones already have installed or you can purchase a compass in the camping department of any discount or sporting goods store. Stand in your front door, point the compass out, and watch the compass needle move. When it stops, turn the compass to align the N (north) with the point on the needle and you have found north. You then will be able to determine the direction your front door faces while looking out your front door by coordinating the direction you are looking with the direction noted on the compass, while keeping the needle point over the N (north).

Next you will need a copy of your home or office's floor plan. If you do not have one, draw a sketch of it. Try to keep the sketch reasonably accurate and keep the rooms in realistic proportions. Be sure to mark the direction your front door faces on your drawing.

Once you have your floor plan and know where north is in relation to your home (or office), you simply lay a copy of the Shape of Life Map over your floor plan, matching the N↔S line on the map with the N↔S line on your compass.

By aligning the map accurately with your compass, you'll be able to determine where the north career section is in your home, along with the other seven areas such as health, relationships, and good luck. You can also place the map over the layout of each room to locate the same areas in each room.

Look at the map and find the areas of concern in your life—the areas where your life is stuck or those which you'd like to improve. Unclutter each of those areas first so that fresh energy can flow. Clutter traps energy, makes it stagnant, and further energizes more clutter. And it can slow down—or completely prevent—good fortune, prosperity, or abundance from entering those areas.

Next, energize those areas as indicated on the map. For example, if you want to improve your relationships, focus positive energy in the southwest area of your home (or your room) using earth tone colors or an earth tone colored number. If those relationships are in the workplace, locate and energize the same area of your office. Or, if you need help finding a new job or selling a home, energize the "helpful people" area in the northwest with something silver or white. You can also display a silver number 6, since you can use the numbers on the Shape of Life Map to energize its specific area. You can also use those numbers in the future to locate your personal number areas and directions.

Summary

Feng Shui truly is a lifestyle. It is about improving your life by using positive energy; eliminating clutter, chaos, and stress; and replacing them with calm, peace, and joy, while honoring your faith, personal convictions, and religious beliefs.

Feng Shui is a vast subject and you can study it for a lifetime without knowing it all. But the beauty of this lifestyle is that it can also be simplified so that it is accessible for everyone. When you work with something simple like a compass and the Shape of Life Map, it takes the confusion out of the process, allowing you to focus on what is most important—creating a better tomorrow.

Get in touch with your true priorities in life so you can eliminate the chaos and stress and allow calm and peace to enter. When calm and peace enter, you've created your own private sanctuary. Once you've created your sanctuary in your personal environment, you learn to nurture yourself and to live a better and more productive life.

To improve and energize your life, start from the outside of your home and work your way in. By starting outside, you can determine if positive energy is reaching your front door. It can then enter and flow throughout your home, depositing vibrant, new positive energy everywhere it travels.

Chapter 3

First Stop: Outside Your Front Door

The exterior of your home is just as important as the interior. People often ask me, "Can I use Feng Shui energy methods outside?" "Should I plant specific colors of flowers to make my yard more peaceful and natural?"

The answer to both questions is a definite yes. The outside of your home, your front door, and your garden need good energy too. In fact, the actual translation of Feng Shui is wind and water. So its roots stem from the outdoors. Here is another rule to keep in mind:

It is critical that the great positive energy moving around the outside of your house can reach your front door, so it can then enter inside.

Wind is a perfect example of positive or negative energy. You can feel the wind when it gently brushes your skin on a warm day, cooling the surface of your body. Yet you can't see it, touch it, or smell it. That type of wind energy is positive.

On the other hand, when wind in the form of a hurricane, tornado, or winter blizzard is approaching, your instincts tell you that danger is coming. That same wind is carrying the negative energy of a storm and you need to protect yourself. Again, you cannot touch the wind, smell it, or see it, yet you know it's approaching. This time, however, it is negative energy. If you don't get out of harm's way, you can see its destructive results.

The same holds true for water. It can be a peaceful lake, a lazy river, or an ocean whose waves gently lap up against the shore. Or, as anyone who's ever been caught at sea when a storm blows in can attest, it can be turbulent and dangerous.

In much the same way, your plantings and garden décor can convey the positive energy of a peaceful, balmy day…or the negative energy of chaos or stormy skies.

Either inside or out, the same Feng Shui principles apply. First, you need to unclutter. Then you need to energize the areas of importance such as relationships, health, prosperity, and abundance using your Shape of Life Map.

Look closely at your front, side, and back yards for overgrown plantings and trees, and then prune and feed them. Also, look for unhealthy plants and bushes. Get rid of them, and replace them with fresh new plantings. The plantings on the outside of your home and on your patio are a direct reflection of the energy surrounding you in other areas of your life. If plantings in the southwest relationships area of your home are unhealthy, your personal relationships may well be the same.

Keep plantings healthy and pruned so that good fortune and prosperity energy will always surround you.

Energize Your Front Yard First

In the field of Feng Shui, your home's front door is perhaps the single most important asset you have…and the obvious place to begin. It is through the front door that most energy, whether positive or negative, enters. Therefore, you'll want to do everything you can to encourage all the positive energy to enter and all the negative to stay away.

Your home's interior may be gorgeous, but you also need fresh, revitalizing energy to enter constantly because that leads to a well-balanced, abundant life. So, how do you ensure the entry of positive energy while preventing negative energy from coming through?

You can achieve this by using a few basic Feng Shui principles, all of which are inexpensive and easy to do. Start by standing in front of your house and observing whether your front door is totally visible. If not, figure out why. Are the plantings overgrown? Is outside clutter blocking the view, such as lawn ornaments or poor-quality lawn furniture? Is the door the same color as your house so it melts into the walls? Is the door on the side of your house, somewhat hidden? If the answer is "yes" to any of the above, you're in luck—you have the power to greatly improve the amount of positive energy that reaches your front door and enters your house.

Improve Your Front Yard Energy by Doing the Following:

- Prune shrubs and plantings to knee-high level so your front entrance is more visible, allowing both energy and guests to find it (and it will also be safer). It's okay to leave a small grouping of taller plantings in this area, such as rhododendron shrubs or palm trees, as long as you can see either through or around them.
- Remove outdoor clutter that prevents good energy from entering. If your "front" door is on the side of the house, use colorful perennials to guide energy to it. Red mulch or a brick edging, for example, would also work well.
- Use colorful plantings that gently curve in and out or up and down to maximize the amount of positive energy arriving at your door, no matter where it is located. Energy will meander through and around the curves slowly until it arrives at your door, carrying with it prosperity and abundance. This is much better than straight lines, where energy shoots right up to the front door then bounces back away from your home.
- To further encourage energy to reach your front door, use a cluster of three or five brightly colored, potted, flowering plants, either real or silk. This is especially important if your door is somewhat hidden in an alcove.
- Hang a small wind chime beside your door. The gentle sound will encourage energy to enter, as well as put gentle, beautiful sounds in your life.

Use gently curving walkways and plantings to ensure positive energy will reach your front door. Positive energy helps you improve health, prosperity, and abundance.

Next, check if neighboring homes or buildings have sharp corners pointing directly at your door. These sharp corners send negative energy toward your home. If possible, you need to either deflect or reverse that energy. Sharp corners include things like fence corners, power poles, cemeteries, factories, and streets that point directly toward your front door or at the front of your entire house, as in a cul-de-sac. To deflect this negative energy, hang a thirty-millimeter, round, ball-shaped, multifaceted, clear crystal in the window nearest the front door or above the door if a window is located there. The crystal should hang down seven inches from the top center of the window. Otherwise, you can also use a small octagon convex mirror to reverse the negative energy. Hang it outside at eye level beside the door on the most exposed side.

Also consider is the color of your front door. Red is often considered to be the "good fortune" color, which is why you often see it on homes and businesses owned by people who understand the energy impact of Feng Shui principles. Green is also considered good for the encouragement of new growth or wealth. But the most helpful energy color for your door really depends on which direction it faces.

Door Color Options Based on the Direction the Door Faces	
East, Southeast, and South	Green or Natural Wood
South and Southwest	Red
West, Northwest, and North	White
North, Northeast, East, and Southeast	Blue

If you live in a home, townhouse, or condo where your neighborhood association determines the exterior colors, you may need to be more creative. Use the previous color and direction guidelines to place flowering plants leading energy to your door. Or find a beautiful large wreath filled with the color that best energizes your front entrance. If you have double-doors, always use a wreath on each door—never put just one on a two-door entrance. At your office or business, place two large pots on either side of the door and fill them with healthy flowering plants in the appropriate color based on the Door Color Options chart. Replace them seasonally as appropriate, or use silk flowers when live ones simply won't work. This will attract positive energy.

By following these suggestions, you'll encourage more positive energy to enter your home and you'll prevent negative energy from entering. A well-energized front door says "Welcome" to the world…and to energy. It also conveys the message of prosperity, good health, and abundance.

First Stop: Outside Your Front Door

Create Outdoor Retreats

The area around your home is an extension of the home itself. Therefore, it should receive the same consideration and treatment for safety, comfort, and energy that you would use inside. This outdoor space should reflect both your personality and your lifestyle, and it should provide you a genuine retreat from the rest of the world. Carefully evaluation your choice of plantings and furniture, as well as their location, and place them so they offer you a pleasing view, proper flow of energy, and a deep sense of relaxation.

When spring arrives, most people turn their thoughts to the great outdoors. Instead of winter's visions of sugarplums dancing in your head, look for flowering daffodils, tulips, and lilacs. It doesn't matter if you live in the sunny South, are still dodging snowflakes in the North, or ending the rainy season out West, spring is the time of year we all dream of new beginnings as we watch the trees burst forth with green plumage. Warm days spent on decks, patios, and in yards are now top of mind.

The arrival of spring brings with it great anticipation of everything new and full of life, abundance, and growth. Many people consider spring the most hopeful time of year because of all the new energy bursting forth from the ground up. However, one of the rites of this season is spring cleaning—gardens need planting, flowerbeds need weeding, and lawn furniture needs restoring.

The glorious attributes of spring can quickly fade if you get caught up in the details of all the work ahead. It can be a lot of work. But in a month or two, you'll reap the benefits. Imagine a perfect summer day relaxing in your outdoor retreat with flowers blooming, birds chirping, and your fountain singing a soothing song. Always keep that vision in mind as you go through the "heavy lifting" to prepare your retreat so you can relax in it once you've completed renewing and revitalizing it.

Five Ways to Energize Your Outdoor Retreat

Once you've decided how big your retreat should be, what it should look like, and how it would best serve you from an energy point of view, consider using these five simple ways to ensure that it flows with positive energy and provides you maximum enjoyment and relaxation:

1. Remove all the unhealthy and dead plantings from winter and replace them with colorful, new ones. Uncluttering provides great new positive energy.
2. Restore to its original beauty and functionality any outdoor furniture. Beauty and safety provide nurturing energy.
3. Replace any furniture and accessories, such as water fountains, if they are not working properly or are broken. New items you love will provide you uplifting energy.
4. Reinvent the reason for your outdoor retreat. It's an extension of your home, your own private outdoor sanctuary, and it will re-energize you.
5. Rekindle traditions and relationships with family and friends while spending time in your outdoor retreat. Old traditions of family and friends gathering for a barbecue or a late-afternoon luau provide great memories for the future and bring back nostalgic and positive energy from the past.

When placing your furniture in your outdoor retreat, preserve the openness and the view. That will also allow energy to flow better. Use gliders and benches in smaller spaces instead of individual chairs. If you can see the back of a piece of furniture from inside your home, make sure it looks nice or camouflage it with a large plant if there is room; if not, add a colorful throw.

To make your retreat more expansive, even in a small yard, you can place a small bench in the opposite corner of the yard, preferably under a tree, to provide an additional mini-sanctuary or focal point. If your retreat doesn't offer enough seclusion for you, you can plant small, bushy trees or make an instant green privacy wall out of large shrubs planted in portable tubs. If your yard is your view and you want it to be your focal point, keep the furniture simple. If the view is not the greatest, invest in nicer furniture and some accessories, such as a fountain, to create the ambiance and view that would otherwise be the missing uplifting energy in your retreat.

Finally, don't forget about the sides of your home. Plant or place primarily neutral plantings in varying sizes and shapes along the sides of your home to prevent energy from zooming right past your home.

As you do the work, whenever you need to, call up the vision of you relaxing in your outdoor retreat. Staying focused on the goal will help you get through the rejuvenating stage peacefully.

Design Patios for Downtime

No matter where you live, the patio, porch, lanai, or deck all provide peaceful, quiet relaxation energy and the opportunity to rest, read a book, and step out of the fast lane. Summer graciously provides you more daylight, so you can enjoy the slower pace of life that sometimes comes with the heat. In order to maximize the relaxation time you spend in your backyard, fill your patio area with slow, meandering energy, rather than energy that zooms through, reminding you of all of the things you have yet to do.

Begin by surrounding yourself with the sounds of refreshing water. The sound of a waterfall is extremely relaxing and revitalizing. You can use anything from a tabletop, self-contained waterfall to a large, elaborate setup with water cascading over several drops and dancing over rocks and flowering tropical plants. The size is not as important as the sound. If you have neither the budget nor the space for an actual waterfall, download some waterfall or bubbling-stream audio files (or purchase CDs) and play them when you are in your relaxation zone. You can even play the sounds of the surf, as it's almost guaranteed to lull you to sleep on a lazy weekend.

Also, consider the use of color when creating a relaxing patio or porch. While you may be tempted to use bright, cheerful, summery colors, realize that those are generally high-energy colors, not quiet, restful ones. Instead, think cool colors like blues, greens, aquas, and teals, as these are the colors of lakes and oceans. These colors are calming as well as cooling on those hot, lazy days of summer. Therefore, outfit your furniture with cushions in a range of these colors to maintain that relaxed feeling. You'll want to spend even more time in your downtime zone when the colors add to a soothing environment.

Plan ahead. As you replace cushions and accessories, think cool, comfortable, and relaxing. Remember to include beverage service and outdoor dinnerware when purchasing cool color accessories. Downtime is important for all of us, as we live in a world that is high pressure, stressful, and invasive. Forget the television and replace the noise pollution with the relaxing sounds of a waterfall. Then just kick back and enjoy your own mini-resort... right in your own backyard.

Here are some additional ideas to create a welcoming backyard sanctuary.

- Flowering plants in the backyard should be pastel in color to promote peaceful energy.
- Hang a few wind chimes, one of which should be made from bamboo as it provides a tranquil sound. These chimes attract peaceful energy.
- If you have a pool, add several groupings of large potted plants in varying sizes. This creates coolness in the summer and helps block the wind in the winter. Cover the dirt in the pots with decorative stones to prevent it from blowing into the pool.

When you have a patio, porch, lanai, or deck, use it. It's great for relaxing, getting rid of stress, and enjoying downtime.

Relaxation and downtime are the ultimate goal of outdoor retreats. Use plants, comfy furniture, and sounds to create your outdoor sanctuary.

Winter Retreat Plans

If you live in a colder climate where you can't use your patio, deck, or porch for part of the year, don't give up on enjoying your outdoor retreat. Bring some of your smaller plantings, and their colorful energy, inside for the winter. Place bird feeders on your decks. The winter birds that come to use them will provide peaceful moments, even during stormy seasons, along with nourishment for the birds.

During the colder months, take time to read books about gardening and browse through those wonderful nursery and garden furniture catalogues so you can make plans for the arrival of next spring. Start your own bedding plants from seeds or plant some outdoor bulbs like tulips, daffodils, and hyacinths indoors and watch them bloom early while the last traces of snow are melting. Then invite friends or family over for an indoor picnic.

Just because it's cold out doesn't mean you have to let go of your summer retreat energy. Whether you simply daydream about last summer and the spring ahead or get busy repairing furniture and planters for the new season, you're keeping the wonderful outdoor retreat energy with you. Think fondly of its nurturing and it will sustain you through the cold weather days.

Enjoy Positive Outdoor Energy All Year Long

Creating positive energy outdoors guarantees better energy will enter your home and life. Be sure lots of fresh, positive energy makes it to—and through—your front door, because that is energy's entrance to both your home and your life. It doesn't matter if your yard is a formal English rose garden, a manicured Japanese garden with a red bridge and water lilies, or a laid-back tropical oasis with palm trees. If the plantings are kept healthy, then positive energy will steadily flow into your personal environment.

Now that you've made sure that positive energy surrounds and enters your home, it's time to move inside and take control of your life. The next chapter provides you a plan on how to energize your home, overcome energy deterrents, and use color, shape and sound to create balance, harmony, and calm.

Chapter 4

Next Stop: Inside Your Front Door

Energy Needs to Meander Throughout

As you open your front door, where does the energy entering go? Is your home's floor plan creating problems because the flow of energy and people is poor? Is great energy entering your front door and then quickly flying out the back door? Does positive energy enter and then immediately run into a wall and have no place to go? These are examples of structural or floor plan flaws built into existing homes that Feng Shui can help you overcome.

Look at your entry way. Once energy reaches your front door, what happens to it? The goal is for it to linger and meander throughout your home, not shoot right through a window or sliding door directly opposite the entrance. Lingering energy is desirable. If it shoots right through, it will take with it any prosperity, abundance, and good health it brought into your home.

Overcoming Structural Flaws

To prevent energy from zooming through your home you can do any of the following:

- Place a circular rug in your entryway to encourage energy to follow the round pattern and circulate throughout your home.
- Place a sofa partway across the room in the direct path of the energy to force it to turn in a different direction.
- Place a sofa table with a beautiful bouquet of flowers or sculpture on it behind the sofa to create a more significant energy barrier.
- Use rug runners to visually shift the directional movement of the energy into different areas of the home.
- Place a small gently flowing tabletop water fountain near the door. The gentle sound and movement will help slow the energy down.

Next Stop: Inside Your Front Door

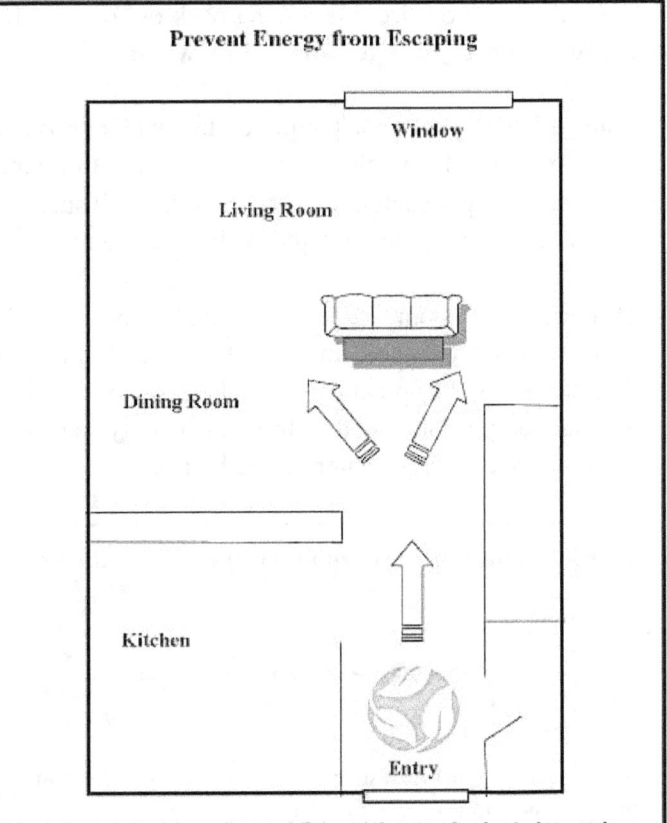

If you open your front door and have a wall directly opposite the door, then you have the reverse problem. The energy does not know where to go and stops or bounces right back out. This is not the place to put a mirror, as it will shoot the energy back out.

To prevent energy from bouncing back out of your front door, you can do any or a few of the following:

- Hang a lovely landscape picture on that wall opposite the door to help welcome the energy and move it through.
- You can also put something clever on the wall such as an arrow showing energy and guests the direction they need to go.
- If there is a room for a small table you can place something on the table that would act as a directional signal, such as a tropical fish, a duck decoy, or a sculpture looking or pointing in the direction energy and guests should move to finish entering the house.

Energizing an Entrance with a Wall Opposite the Door

· Use expansive pictures, such as a landscape, opposite your door to encourage energy to enter.
· Direct the energy and guests into your home by placing interesting signage on the wall or tabletop.
· Use a duck decoy or some other animal to point the way into your home.

Is the kitchen the first room upon entering your home or easily accessed from the front door? The kitchen is the heart of your home and must be guarded from energy rushing right through, taking your abundance away with it. If the kitchen is the first thing you see upon entering your home and the last thing you see upon leaving it, you will always be thinking about food, which can be bad energy for your diet. If there is no wall or counter between the kitchen and front door, try maintaining some type of divider between the spaces even if it is a half wall or a grouping of tall plants and silk trees.

Is there a bathroom right in the middle of your home or very near the front door? This is another potential problem area. Not only will the energy entering your home rush right into the bathroom, but it will go right down the drain, taking your prosperity and good luck with it. If possible, relocate the bathroom door so it faces a direction other than the front door or kitchen. If that is not possible, always keep that bathroom door closed, the toilet seat down, and the sink drain closed so the good energy will not go down the drain but rather meander throughout the house and help create abundance and prosperity.

Home Décor Can Prevent Energy Movement

Structural flaws occur all the time and are quite easy to overcome. Sometimes, however, what you put into a house prevents energy from gently flowing in and out of every room. Home décor problem solving usually just takes a little time and effort.

Make sure all rooms that are in view when the front door is opened are totally clutter-free and nothing is preventing energy from gently moving throughout. Remove stacks of "stuff," magazines, and boxes.

Start by getting rid of "stuff" that you've allowed to pile up for days, weeks, and years. For example, do you procrastinate folding your laundry so stacks of it sit around for weeks on end? Do you have "I'll get to it someday" piles of papers and magazines, yet "someday" never comes? Are you a "saver of everything" because you might need it someday? Sort it, file it, keep what is important, and get rid of everything else.

When you declutter, you'll find that it's so much easier to clean your rooms, and you'll be amazed at how much larger your rooms seem without all that "stuff" on your floors, countertops, and tables. See the Calm Your Chaos section for more on uncluttering.

Remove large obstacles from the path energy would naturally take and replace those items with smaller, circular shaped or curved items; energy will flow around the smaller things. If energy travels quickly down a long hallway and does not enter rooms on either side of the hallway, use a floor runner with a slightly wavy pattern or geometric shapes to slow the energy down. You can also place pictures along the hallway at varying heights and in varying sizes to slow the energy down so it has time to enter all rooms.

Eliminate too many pillows, throws, and dustables. Get rid of furniture that is too dirty to clean or badly worn if you cannot slipcover it. Eliminate unnecessary pieces. For example, do you really need three old sofas in one small living room? Get rid of anything you do not want or need. The energy entering your home will be able to meander freely and you will feel calm and in control.

Avoid dark areas anywhere in your house where stagnant negative energy gathers. Whether it is a dark long hallway, a small dark back entry from a garage, a stairwell, or even a room with little or no natural light, make sure there is always light moving through those areas. Paint walls in those areas a light color. Add overhead lighting that is controlled by a wall switch, or place a lamp in those areas on a timer so the light automatically turns on at dusk and off at a predetermined time later. The added lighting not only ensures energy will move properly through those areas, but will also provide you safety when walking through them.

Next, open your curtains and shades to let all the glorious sunshine energy into your home. The sun's energy through light and heat is wonderful for cleansing and healing. Too often we close our curtains and blinds for days on end to keep the sun out when we should bask in its wonderful nurturing energy.

If you live in a hot climate and are concerned about the sun fading furniture and rugs, make a habit of opening all of your curtains first thing in the morning. As the sun moves and beams into certain windows, close only those curtains for the few hours of sun. You can keep northern-facing windows open all the time unless you need to close them for privacy. In the cooler and more moderate climates, you can leave your curtains open all day until summer arrives.

Is the Energy Still Stuck?

Do you and your house still feel out-of-sorts after remedying any structural issues? Do you notice something is not quite right when you walk into certain rooms of your home? Do you sometimes wonder whether your furnishings and colors are contributing to your lack of well-being? These are the feelings that occur when a home is out of balance.

Do you tend to avoid certain rooms? Have you rearranged your bedroom and are not sleeping well? Are there certain chairs in your home you never sit in? These are clues that something is out of balance. No matter where you are in your home you should feel comfortable, calm, and contented.

Pretend you are a first-time visitor to your home. Walk in the front door and through your home room by room, observing with your eyes plus feeling internally what happens when you enter each room. Do you feel welcome and comfortable, or do you want to leave immediately?

As soon as you notice something uncomfortable, stop and carefully analyze what is causing the discomfort. Make a note of what you observed.

- Is the room cluttered everywhere or in a certain area?
- Are the predominant colors in the room dark and dreary or are they too bright and loud?
- Are the furnishings in that room extremely angular, hard, and shiny or are they rounded, soft, and dull?
- Is the room overcrowded with furniture or is it too sparse?

Each of the above scenarios will create an imbalance in your home and give you that out-of-sorts feeling. Additionally, it will hinder your well-being.

Check every area where you feel discomfort to find the cause. Yes, it could be as simple as clutter. If so, get rid of those stacks of magazines and newspapers, old books you will never read, boxes of pictures you never look at, and closets full of clothes you never wear. Stacks of boxes filled with "stuff" are a sure sign of years of clutter.

If you never look at pictures, read the books and magazines, or wear the clothes, what value do they have? They've become stagnant negative energy. This one step of uncluttering will encourage fresh new energy to enter your home and increase its flow throughout.

If you've recently rearranged the furniture in a room and it doesn't feel comfortable but was before you moved it, put it back. If you haven't moved furniture in a long time, move some of the pieces so energy can flow throughout more freely. As you move things, do not leave the backs of chairs or sofas exposed, as it creates negative energy for the person sitting there. If chairs do not sit up against a wall or in a corner, place them so that anyone sitting there can observe others entering and leaving the room. Or, place a long slender sofa table with a statue or large silk plants behind the sofa to create security for those sitting there.

If you do not like sitting in a specific chair, look at how it is positioned in your room. Sitting in a chair with its back exposed or toward a door is unnerving and uncomfortable.

Now, look at the colors in each room and the shape of the furniture. Is the room dark or filled with mostly earth tone colors and soft furniture with lots of curves? This may be providing you depressing, discouraging, and discomforting energy. You will need to lighten it up. Use a torchiere lamp that sends light upward, add some brighter colors, and include one or two pieces of angular furniture.

If the room is too angular or white with uncomfortable furniture, this energy will make you tense and irritable. Provide more soft furniture and earth tones on the walls to tone it down.

Color, Shape, and Sound

Once you have completed correcting the structural flaws and additional ones created by furnishings and belongings, it is time to add color, shape, and sound to assist the flow of energy. Apply this formula to your home and office:

C + S + S = BS (Color + Shape + Sound = Balanced Surroundings)

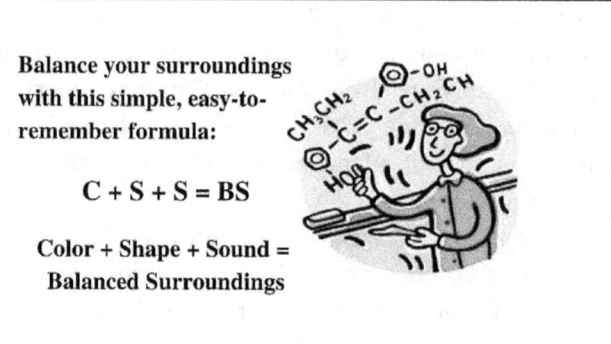

Balance your surroundings with this simple, easy-to-remember formula:

C + S + S = BS

Color + Shape + Sound = Balanced Surroundings

Your eyes and ears are truly your windows to the world. Positive colors, shapes, and sounds in Feng Shui design will bring harmony, balance, and positive energy into your world.

- Color, shape, and sound are the most prevalent influences in our society other than people and television.
- Color, shape, and sound can make you happy, sad, depressed, or agitated.
- Each color, shape, and sound has its own unique energy and its own unique influence on the way you feel.

Color

According to the Interior Design Industry and Paint Manufacturers, people like color in their homes to have similar values of the lights and darks found in nature. Their research shows that sixty to seventy-five percent of the colors with which we surround ourselves need to be warm, light colors (cream, soft yellow, taupe, peach, pink, lilac, earth tones, and such) and twenty-five to forty percent need to be cool colors (greens and blues).

We find the warmer colors of nature more desirable and soothing than the cooler colors, such as the blues of the sky and water. Our most peaceful surroundings come from the use of colors found in nature, in the proportions above. So, if you're looking to create a more peaceful atmosphere in your home or office, think of the palette Mother Nature provided.

If, on the other hand, you're looking to liven up your energy, think brighter colors. Generally, according to the researchers, Americans like their color in sixty-thirty-ten proportions: sixty percent of our homes and offices have light, neutral colors on the walls and floors, thirty percent are in various hues in our furnishings, and the remaining ten percent are in bright accent colors.

We feel comfortable when we use colors in these general proportions because they are similar to what nature surrounds us with. It's when we move out of those comfort ranges and go into one-color rooms (walls, furniture, floors, and accents in the same color or values) or a dark color on one or all four walls, that we find ourselves feeling blue, down, or even anxious and aggravated.

When rooms are all one color, you take on the energy of the monochromatic color of that room, causing unbalance because you are missing the energy of the other colors. In a room where one wall is a different color, the energy that normally meanders throughout stops when it reaches a different-colored wall, becoming confused and not knowing whether it should retreat or move on. Energy becomes stagnant or stuck because the different color prevents it from moving on.

Take a close look at your home to see whether you are working within the simple sixty-thirty-ten ratio. If the answer is "yes," then you should have relatively balanced surroundings where you get neither anxious nor depressed. On the other hand, if you're feeling lethargic, un-energized, un-motivated, aggravated, or aggressive, you really need to look closely at your surroundings and evaluate why. You may come to the realization that it's time to brighten things up or tone them down.

The following color chart provides some general information on a sampling of color basics. While there are many shades of each color, such as celery, mint, and sage variation of green, the information still applies. The chart is a compilation of data from the interior design field, the paint manufacturing field, and the Encyclopedia of Educational Technology.

Color Basics Chart

Color	Energy Type	Traits/Uses
Red	Dangerous Exciting	High arousal color, conveys charged emotions like anger, love, and passion. Use it in small amounts as an accent in public rooms like the kitchen, living room, and family room. It is best to not use it in bedrooms. Do not use it in any area where you eat, as it increases your appetite and passion for the indulgence of food.
Yellow	Optimism Anxiety	Least popular hue in the color spectrum, stimulates memory, the nervous system, and internal organs. Associated with high-pitched sounds, sour smells, heat, and triangles. Not easy to look at for extended periods of time. Use it in limited amounts. Do not use pure yellow in nurseries.
Blue	Calm	Non-threatening, neutral, and the color of trust, longevity, and dependability. It induces a calming effect and lowers blood pressure. Blue strengthens the immune and nervous systems and increases a sense of security for children. Can be used in any room but too much can be cold and depressing for some. Do not use it in the kitchen as it makes food look devoid of nutrients.

Orange	Uplifting	Brightest color in the spectrum, use it sparingly unless toned down. It is associated with earth tones and grounding and can cheer you up. Use peach or flesh tones on walls, as it encourages joy and happiness. Orange makes a great accent in the brighter shades. It is a youthful color that pleases the inner child.
Green	New Healthy Natural	Evokes a sense of relaxation, comfort, and quietness. It is the easiest color for the eye to see and the most restful. Green is associated with spring, new growth, and new beginnings. Holding rooms in theaters and studios are painted green because of its calming effect. It reflects love, harmony, peace, and goodwill toward others. It provides mental and physical equilibrium and is great for stress. It can be used abundantly throughout a home in light to medium values.
Purple & Violet	Thoughtful Reflective	A somewhat serious meditative color long associated with royalty, luxury, and religious holidays as well as spirituality. It is a balance of red and blue that creates introspective energy. In pastel shades it can be used on walls and in darker shades makes a great accent for most rooms.

Pink	Calm Romance	Associated with sweetness and innocence, feminine and softness, pink is the most used color for candy and girls' bedrooms and clothing. In the right shade, it is also used in prison cells to calm prisoners. It can be used in lighter shades on walls and in brighter shades as accents in most rooms.
Brown	Neutrality Self-Control	This is the ultimate earth color and provides grounded, stable, and calm energy. It is also associated with wild animals. When used in light colors such as tan it is a very comfortable color in all rooms. Too much dark brown can be depressing.
Black	Formality Introspection	It can be a passive uncommunicative color in home décor and a little goes a long way. It is not a good color in rooms where you want pleasant conversations and to encourage good relationships. It is best used as an accent or for dramatic effects.
White	Purity Cleanliness	It is thought of as a cold, distant, and sharp or unfriendly color yet sterile and clean. It is also thought of as a color of purity and peace. While it is a common color, softer versions of white tinted slightly with some of the above colors make it a more user-friendly and enjoyable color, especially in rooms where people need to interact on a friendly basis regularly.

Shape

Similar percentages and rules found in the colors section apply to shapes and textures, such as curvy and soft versus straight and hard. Our society generally prefers a larger percentage of soft lines and curves to harsh, straight lines and hard surfaces. If you want to create a peaceful environment, create a ratio of sixty percent soft and curvy to forty percent hard lines and surfaces in your home. The opposite holds true in an office where you need higher productive energy.

You will find a lot of basic information about shapes and lines in the Demystifying Feng Shui chapter under the Yin/Yang and Elements sections. The information below will provide you additional descriptions on the energy various shapes provide.

To obtain the desire energy when using shapes and lines, refer to the following guidelines.

Desired Energy	Shapes and Lines	Where to Use
High	Triangles, pyramids, diamonds, starbursts found in things like brass containers, chrome objects, electronic equipment	Workout rooms, offices, but very little elsewhere
Comforting Nurturing	Horizontal shapes, heavy objects, soft fabrics found in upholstered furniture, curtains, rugs, wooden tables	Common areas such as family, dining or living rooms and bedrooms
Strong and Sharp	Circular and long slender shapes, found in items like mirrors, metal objects, furniture without upholstery, televisions, and rooms with no window treatments	Offices but not bedrooms and only smaller amounts in other rooms

Inspiration/ Spiritual	Wavy and fluid shapes; for relaxation, universal and individual consciousness	All rooms, especially good in rooms you want quiet
Growth Renewal	Vertical, rectangular shapes found in wooden furniture; plants	All rooms

Use the preceding energy descriptions for shapes to help you balance your rooms and support the activities that take place in those rooms. For example, in a family room where you want interaction with others, use the soft, comfortable, rounded shapes and upholstered furniture to encourage comfort and conversation. You would balance that with a limited number of the high energy shapes by using items like electronic equipment or a tall brass touchier lamp. For an office where work needs to take place efficiently, you would reverse this process.

Sound

Over the last thirty to fifty years, numerous universities, research teams, and businesses in the United States, Canada, and Great Britain have conducted much research on sound. They primarily focused on noise pollution created by airplanes, equipment like jackhammers, traffic, and even loud learning centers to study the negative impact it has on everyone from infants to the elderly. The research shows that the negative effects of noise pollution include:

- Damage to hearing
- Elevated blood pressure
- Learned helplessness
- Lowered motivation
- Less tolerance and more frustration
- Poorer reading and academic skills in children

There is even more written on sound in the form of music and its effects on humans. While some research reveals the negative impact of specific types of music, as well as the harm caused by loud amplification, most of the research focuses on the well-being benefits of music.

Topping the list as the most beneficial type of music were specific pieces of classical music as well as New Age or sound healing music. The classical ranged from several compositions of Mozart to Bach and Handel. The reason given for the success of these pieces was that the tempo of the music closely correlates to the human heartbeat and lacked a strong percussion element.

The New Age music, once considered to be outside the traditional music industry, is composed specifically to nurture the body, mind, and spirit. Often referred to as music to support balance and harmony in the body, New Age music offers a full spectrum of expressive sound as a powerful new language of feeling through rhythm, harmony, and sound energy.

Research shows that listening to the right type of music at an appropriate volume can:

- Improve self-perception and raise self-esteem
- Reduce anxiety and lower pain
- Evoke a feeling of calm and relaxation

- Increase creativity
- Accelerate learning
- Enhance spatial IQ
- Increase short- and long-term memory

Sound, especially music, is just as important as shape and color when it comes to balancing your home and your personal well-being. Sound privacy from noise pollution and the choice of the music you listen to should provide you both listening pleasure plus support and nurture you.

As you embark on your Feng Shui journey, remember the formula C + S + S = BS and apply it. It will improve your balance and harmony and lead you to creating calmness where chaos exists.

Chapter 5

Calm Your Chaos

You may still be wondering, "Will Feng Shui help me?" "Will it make a difference in my life?" "Will it make my life better than it is right now?" "Can I regain control of my life?" "Can I get rid of the chaos and create calm?" "Will it make my life better tomorrow than it is today?" These are questions people ask all the time.

Isn't that what everyone wants—a better, more peace-filled, and less stressful life? A life where you are in control rather than other people or circumstances? A life where you are surrounded by calm rather than chaos?

When your life is not in balance, you are in varying degrees of chaos and may feel uncomfortable and unfocused. But you can create balance from chaos and attain peace within. Whether you are looking to improve your health, your relationships, your income, or your overall well-being, Feng Shui will make a difference. It really works.

Chaos Creates Negative Energy

The Chinese developed the lifestyle concept of Feng Shui to create and maintain a balanced and peaceful life. They maximized the use of good energy in their lives so they could be healthier, more prosperous, and enjoy life.

Feng Shui is a way to energize your world and help you find more balance in your life. In our high stress, multitasking world we continually face unrest, chaos, and physical threats. It is important that our homes be our sanctuary from the outside world. When your life is completely balanced, you eliminate chaos and experience more joy, hope, and peace.

Positive energy can come into your life in many forms—good health, prosperity, and good friends, to name a few. Feng Shui is the use of positive energy in yourself and your surroundings to bring about desired results, such as reducing stress so you can create calm or eliminating clutter so you can become more focused and productive. It's that simple.

One of the most desirable results is that you can learn to be in control of yourself and your personal environment. The best way to do that is to surround yourself with positive energy. When you remove the stagnant energy and clutter that are creating the chaos in your world and replace them with positive, supportive energy, you will soon find yourself—and your surroundings—balanced, revitalized, and at peace.

You create positive or negative energy based on what you surround yourself with, in your home and in your workplace. Every thing and every thought has energy that is either positive and serves you well or negative and serves you adversely. If you surround yourself with belongings, furnishings, and items you love, they'll bring you supportive and positive energy. If you have furniture, belongings, and items in your home or office that you don't like, they will generate negative energy. The more negative energy you have in your life, the more chaotic and out of control it will be. Again, this is all very simple to accomplish.

Every time you look at your overflowing kitchen and bathroom counters, you get a reminder of all the work you still have left to do. When you sit at your desk and see that it's covered with papers and files, you feel overwhelmed before you begin. If you have stacks of books or magazines by your bed waiting to be read, your subconscious mind continues to dwell upon all of the unfinished tasks and projects you still have ahead of you. Chances are you're not getting a restful night's sleep under these conditions. Stacks of anything in your bedroom prevent you from sleeping soundly.

Calm Your Chaos with a Plan

How do you deal with the years of stuff you've collected, inherited, or have been given by well-meaning friends and relatives? One of the most successful ways to handle this is to make a plan, take action, and then revisit the plan every six months. But make sure the plan is simple…or your good intentions will not overcome the fear of letting go.

When creating your plan, the best place to begin is your bedroom. Sleep—restorative, restful sleep—is important every night in order to regenerate and re-energize your body for the next day. It's hard enough to face piles of things that need your daily attention when you're well-rested; when you're tired, facing those things can seem like an impossible task.

The Bedroom

This plan is easier than you think. Begin with your closets and drawers. Get three large boxes. Label the first one "donate," the second "toss," and the third "maybe." Everything in your closet that does not pass the *"I love it; it looks great on me and I feel terrific in it"* test gets put into one of these three boxes. If an item can't pass this simple test, do not put it back into your closet! Those pieces are negative energy for you, preventing you from moving forward or letting go of things you should have released years ago.

Find a permanent home—either hanging in the closet or folded in drawers—for what you're keeping before moving on. Everything else should wind up in one of the three boxes and be disposed of properly.

Important: Place only a few things into the "maybe" box and review the contents of that box in six months. If you still are not sure at that time, toss or donate the items. Someone else will fall in love with the things that no longer give you positive energy. You'll find more positive energy information for your wardrobe in the It Matters What You Wear chapter.

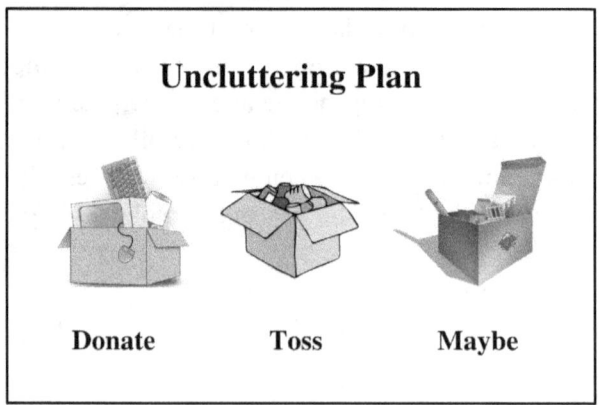

When you have finished the closet, take a close look at the remainder of the room. Clothing is not the only thing that creates clutter in a bedroom. Clutter can be anything from stacks of books, boxes, and magazines to an excessive number of pillows, throws, and dustables. Even electronic equipment and computers fit this definition of clutter in a bedroom.

Clutter in the bedroom causes stress and stands in the way of a peaceful night's sleep. It can even create friction between you and your significant other. Clutter in your relationship area will cause chaos in your relationships. It will cause unwanted constant little health issues for you and your family if it is in your health area, and little improvement in monetary growth if in your income area. Therefore, when eliminating clutter, get rid of it; don't just move it to another room.

Once you've eliminated the clutter, the five guidelines below will help you ensure proper rest, rejuvenation, and more energized relationships.

- Place your bed as far from the door as possible and avoid having your feet point out the door while sleeping. This location maximizes safety and ensures proper rest. Store nothing under your bed so rejuvenating energy can gently flow around you while sleeping. Be sure you have a headboard attached to your bed to support you and provide you maximum rest. The bed placement diagram below is appropriate for adults and children.

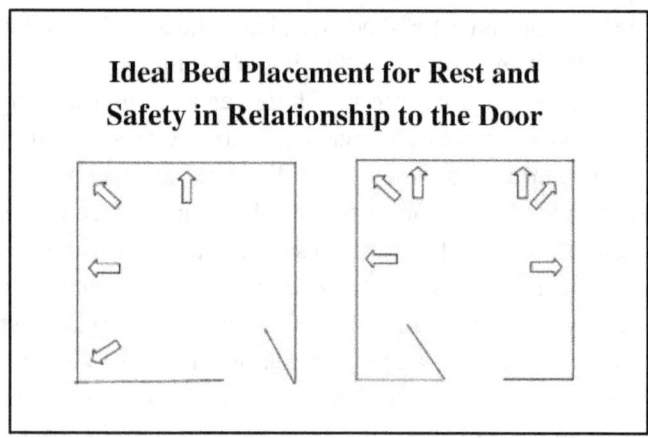

- Choose soothing wall colors in soft pastels to promote restorative rest and relaxation. Linens should also be calming colors with limited pattern. Soft blues and pinks provide calming energy, pastel greens promote good health energy, and light earth tones provide healthy relationships energy. For more information on color, see the Color Section in the Next Stop: Inside the Front Door chapter.

- Hang only those pictures on bedroom walls that depict love, showcase calming scenery, or represent where you want your personal life to be in the future. If you want to get married or improve your marriage, hang pictures of loving couples or things in pairs. If you want the bedroom to be less stress-filled, hang pictures of a gentle stream or a pastoral landscape. A word of caution, the bedroom is not the place to hang pictures of parents, children, or other loved ones. All those eyes watching you can be quite disconcerting and not conducive to rest and intimacy.

- Remove all exercise and electronic equipment such as computers from the bedroom. They are high-energy pieces whether in use or not and demand attention. Your subconscious mind will not rest properly when it is constantly reminded of work to be done or exercise that is needed. If you must have a television in the bedroom, place it in a wardrobe and close the doors when it is not in use.

- In the southwest area of your bedroom, energize your relationships by adding a vase with two beautiful flowers of equal size and value matching your room décor. You may also use something like a pair of turtle doves or two giraffes with their necks intertwined.

Bedroom Sanctuary

- **Clutter-free**
- **Positioned as far from the door as possible**
- **Solidly grounded with an attached headboard**
- **Pastel calming colors on walls**

Yes, it really is that easy to create a stress-free bedroom sanctuary that nurtures you and a loving relationship while providing your body physical rest and ample positive energy to rejuvenate.

Once you have uncluttered and energized your bedroom, not only have you taken care of some early-spring or fall cleaning in your bedroom, but you'll also rest much better and wake up feeling more refreshed.

The Kitchen

Next, move on to your kitchen. In terms of Feng Shui, the kitchen is the second most important room and source of positive energy in your home. Think of the kitchen as the heart of the home. Everything, including your good health, productivity, and abundance, gets its start in your kitchen. Whether you are a master chef and love to cook, a take-out connoisseur, or a frequent restaurant patron doesn't matter. What does matter is realizing that your kitchen is important when it comes to your prosperity and abundance.

It's difficult to prepare meals when you're faced with mounds of junk mail, jackets, lunch boxes, grocery bags, pet supplies, and dirty dishes, just to name a few obstacles. Ideally, keep your kitchen counters as empty and clean as possible to allow for the maximum flow of positive energy.

Following are three steps to creating great energy in your kitchen—the kind of energy that stays with you and nurtures you every day of the week.

Step 1: Unclutter

Create a clutter-free kitchen and eliminate the chaos to allow fresh new energy to meander throughout. This will create room for good health, wealth, and abundance to enter your life. Unclutter by cleaning out your food pantry and discarding anything that is no longer fresh or you will never eat. Follow the same process in your refrigerator. Maintain some empty space to allow for new foods and new energy to enter your life.

Move on to your cupboards and drawers. Eliminate anything that is cracked, chipped, broken, never-to-be-used, or a duplicate item or appliance. If you're not going to use it or it's broken, *get rid of it!*

Now that the inside of your cupboards is uncluttered, do the same on the countertops. Counters need to remain clutter-free for nurturing energy to meander unobstructed and the preparation of food—even if the food is only a cup of coffee on the run or a take-out meal.

If you have small children in your home, the kitchen walls and refrigerator often tend to be a place to display all their wonderful artwork and creations. While displaying one or two pieces provides positive family energy, an entire wall or fully-covered refrigerator creates stagnant and disjointed energy. This can lead to not wanting to be in the kitchen to prepare meals, total distraction for the food preparer, or not enjoying a meal when sitting nearby. Limit the creativity and pictures to the most recent one for each child and find another special place to use as a creativity gallery.

Step 2: Organize

Organize your kitchen so it is convenient, functional, and productive. Doing so will save you time, steps, and personal energy, which leads to less stress, better health, and improved productivity. Start with determining how to deal with trash and garbage. Since garbage is decaying, life–draining, stagnant energy, as soon as possible place it into the appropriate trash containers and recycle bins. If you keep your garbage in the kitchen to be removed later, keep it in a closed container or enclosed in a cupboard.

Organize your pantry with baskets or bins so you know immediately when you are about to run out of supplies. Follow this same process in your refrigerator. When you are running low on an item, place it on a shopping list to purchase on your next trip to the grocery store.

Place any appliances not used regularly into the cupboards or nearby closet and return them to the countertop only when needed. Place all knives and tools with sharp points in drawers, putting them out of sight and reach and providing good safety protection energy.

By organizing, you are calming the chaos that lingers in kitchens. As a result, you will be more efficient and you will enjoy your newfound energy and calm.

Step 3: Energize

I saved this step for last so that you don't inadvertently energize the clutter, creating even more chaos and blocking new energy from entering. Use some of the following to energize your health, wealth, abundance, and prosperity.

- Place a bowl of fresh fruit on your kitchen table or countertop. Good-looking faux fruit will also work. This energizes abundance.
- Keep your refrigerator stocked with nourishing foods. This energizes prosperity.

Always maintain your refrigerator as full as possible to energize prosperity. Place a bowl of fruit on either your kitchen counter or table to energize abundance.

- Keep your stove top spotlessly clean and rotate the use of your burners. The stove is referred to as the wealth energizer in your kitchen.
- Having your back to a door or entrance to your kitchen provides you negative unsettling energy from behind. Place a shiny pot, mirror, or reflective artwork on your stove, counter, or wall in front of you so you can see anyone approaching. This will prevent you from being startled or accidentally hurting yourself with a knife or hot burner.

X marks the spot.
If your back is toward the entrance to your kitchen while cooking, place a shiny piece of art, a pot, or a mirror in front of you to prevent being startled and causing an accident.

- Your kitchen is an important energy provider in your personal environment. By uncluttering it, organizing it, and energizing it, you are encouraging positive new energy to freely meander through. This energy leads to improved health, prosperity, and abundance—and will get your day off to a productive and successful start every morning.

Dispose of things like junk mail immediately. At the same time, always place bills and letters in baskets or drawers designated for just that purpose, so they're easily accessible. Find ways that work best for dealing with dishes, groceries, and all of the other things that tend to accumulate on your counters. Baskets work well for organizing the kitchen. (They're also great in the bathroom and the office.)

As far as method, the same rules that apply to the bedroom apply to the kitchen. If it's cracked, chipped, or rusty, or if you haven't used it in three years or have more than one, *get rid of it!*

Complete Your Calming Plan

Move to the bathroom, and then the rest of your home. Use all the same guidelines in your plan from one room to the next. Don't forget the basement, attic, and garage.

If you have young children, create an area of a room or a closet just for them. Fill it with lots of containers and cabinets with little drawers to store all those little toy parts, accessories, crayons, chalk, pencils, and scissors. Organize this area frequently so it stays uncluttered. This will also help children learn the importance of caring for their things and uncluttering at an early age.

Here are some additional guidelines to help you remove the stagnant energy of clutter, calm your chaos, and bring positive energy into your world.

- "If you don't love it, get rid of it." Apply this rule to everything that surrounds you, except for those things that are needed and functional.
- Of course, keep one or two of those special letters from parents, grandparents, and loved ones. Consider framing them or placing them into a memories box to honor their importance. Then eliminate the rest. It's nice to remember loved ones, but it's not helpful to keep your energy tied to the past.
- When it comes to magazines, unless they are saleable or a collector's edition, get rid of them. You may want to clip some articles as reference materials, for example future vacation sites. If so, organize and file these clippings immediately. Or you may choose to keep a few magazines that record historical events through the years, but then get rid of the rest. You can give them to a charitable

- organization where they can be used for a fund-raiser or a paper drive, or simply recycle them.
- If you're constantly losing things for projects, whether in the garage, the office, or the sewing room, keep a small box in each of those areas and label it for the specific project for which they're needed. Every time you buy additional items for that project, toss them into that same box.
- If you buy software for your computer, keep all the software information, CDs or thumb drives, and programs in one well-labeled box so you know exactly where to look when you need to reference it.
- Create a similar well-labeled box to hold all your appliances' instruction manuals, warranties, and purchase information such as date and location of purchase. This will save you time when you need repairs done as well as when selling your home. You will want to leave a number of these items with the house for the new owner.

Remember: An easy rule to follow with "stuff" is:

If you haven't used it in the last three years, if it's broken, chipped or rusty, or is an unnecessary duplicate get rid of it!

Removing clutter from your world not only energizes you and your home, but it also makes your life so much easier! You no longer have to dust it or clean around it. You no longer trip over it when getting out of your car in the garage. And you now have extra space in your closet for a new outfit that will make you feel and look great for that upcoming special event in your life.

Letting go of years of accumulated things not only clears out closets, bedrooms, the attic, and the garage, but also clears the cobwebs out of your head so you can deal with all of the new things you get bombarded with every day. There's nothing magical about all items we collect or hold onto. Letting go of things energizes the house (and workplace), makes it roomier and more comfortable, and helps you let go of the past.

Create a Sanctuary for Peace

As noted in the Sound section of the Next Stop: Inside Your Front Door chapter, sound pollution is one of the curses of the twenty-first century. Whether you recognize it as a major pollutant in your personal environment or not, you need to deal with it. These days, sound pollution intrudes on virtually every aspect of our lives, often in places we used to think of as quiet. It's difficult to find peace in a world of impersonal cement cities and isolated environments created by cubicles, television, and electronic games. Each of us needs to be alert and acknowledge this for what it is—a threat to our peace within.

Sound pollution comes in many forms. It can be from the obvious, such as televisions, cell phones, and blaring car horns. Or it can come from less obvious sources, such as the hum of fluorescent lighting, computers, and air conditioners or furnaces.

The good news is that you can overcome the ever-present invasive sound pollution by creating a little sanctuary just for yourself in a quiet spot in your home. It can be a comfortable chair or a small desk and chair in your bedroom, a guest room, or the sun porch. When you're in this spot, have only a pencil and paper handy so you can jot down notes while using your sanctuary. Be sure to be absolutely still for at least fifteen minutes while sitting in your sanctuary, and use it at least twice a week. You can meditate while in this space, visualize peaceful settings, write in a journal, or simply stare out a window or at the flame of a burning candle.

Make sure everything is quiet so you can hear yourself think and your subconscious mind can communicate with you. Write down only thoughts that are new, refreshing, and filled with positive energy that you should act on. *Then act on them!* Those thoughts will lead your choices that make every day count. Don't be afraid to remind family members that your sanctuary time is sacred and you are not to be disturbed. Also, don't fall into the trap of letting the telephone, television, or doorbell distract you. You deserve and need absolute silence.

Create a Sanctuary

When you need a dose of "calm" to control the chaos around you but you're not able to be in your sanctuary, play some peaceful music to create that calm. There are several wonderful CDs or music download options that range from Feng Shui and Zen to melodic piano and violin music. There's no one magic bullet for everyone. Find the music that provides you the most peace. And save it for those days you are really in need. See the Resources page for well-being music.

Positive Energy Provides Desired Results

By uncluttering your world, you'll calm much of your chaos. When you apply the formula using color, shape, and sound, you'll complete the process of balancing your surroundings. And by creating a sanctuary, you'll have a peace-filled environment. Your personal world will be filled with positive supportive energy. You'll live a better life and enjoy it abundantly.

Now that you've learned how to take control of your surroundings and calm in your world, it's time to turn your attention to the people and relationships in your life and learn ways to eliminate negative thinking, regenerate and store positive energy, and create an Intentions Board to accomplish your goals.

Chapter 6

Do You Have the Relationships You Want?

Ending old relationships, or beginning new ones, can be challenging...and very upsetting. However, beginning again can also be uplifting and rewarding because you're sweeping out the old, for whatever reason, and bringing in the new. New energy, in the form of repairing or ending old relationships or beginning new ones, is always positive.

The ideal relationship is a balanced one, where each person gives and receives energy equally. If a person's life is not balanced, then their relationship energy will also be unbalanced. Some individuals may be very needy and always draining your energy, pushing themselves on you or demanding your time. Others may be constantly giving you their time, their opinions, and their gifts, which can be a more passive form of control. Both are forms of needy energy...just at the opposite ends of the equation.

So, how do you shift the energy in a relationship? Is there a way to begin new relationships, or repair old ones, and shift energy without totally changing your life?

By creating balance in your personal environment—and getting rid of chaos caused by the negative energy in your life—Feng Shui principles will help you create a lifestyle filled with a positive flow of energy that is conducive to generating the kind of relationships you want and deserve.

Life Is All about Relationships

No matter where you are or what you are doing, a relationship is involved. When you buy groceries, you interact with a cashier. When you go to the doctor, you interact with the receptionist, a nurse, a doctor, and possibly more people. When you go to a restaurant, you interact with the server. Whether you're interacting with someone for one hour, one day, or one year, you need to shift all relationship energy to positive, supportive, or helpful energy. You'll be amazed at how much more pleasant your life will be once you do this.

You can begin slowly to renew your relationships and your thinking, or you can go full speed ahead. Either way, there are specific things you can do to achieve the relationships you really want. It's not hard to start anew and make a real difference in your life.

Most people live their life in a very routine manner. But the more you live your life according to the habits you have fallen into, the less likely it is that new positive energy will enter, and the less observant you'll be about the energy in your long-standing relationships. Also, because you're allowing less new energy to enter, it's more difficult to re-kindle or revitalize old relationships.

Define Your Relationships

Before you can have and enjoy the relationships you really want, you must understand the different types of relationships. All the relationships listed below are interactive relationships but require different energy support.

You and Yourself

The first and most important relationship you need to be aware of is the one you have with yourself. If you love yourself and respect yourself, you'll find it easier to have equal and balanced relationships with others. We seem to have become a culture of "dumbing down" the importance of self-respect and balance in our lives. This has a profound impact on how we value life…in this case, your relationship with yourself.

Adult to Adult

This are relationships you choose or are born into, such as a spouse, friends, adult family members, and parents once you reach adulthood. Ideally, these relationships have balanced support for each other and respect the independence of each person—a balance that supports the right of each person to have their own opinions, without imposing their ideals upon the others.

Parent/Child

In this case, the adult is responsible for caring for, nurturing, and teaching the child. The adult has the responsibility to raise the child to become a successful adult who can care themselves and contribute positive energy to society. You may be interested to know that both the parent and the child share energy responsibility in this relationship. But—make no mistake—the parent should be the one who's in charge.

Business and Professional Relationships

A relationship in this category is generally filled with people with whom you might not otherwise be associated, such as those in the workplace, the gym, the grocery store, organizations to which you belong, or with professionals such as doctors, attorneys, and accountants. These relationships are usually mandatory or obligatory, and can become major energy-drainers when not properly nurtured.

Helpful People

The interactions involved here aren't truly relationships as we commonly think of them. These are supportive energy relationships. An example would be a family referring a potential new client to their realtor because their realtor helped them with many details at a very busy time in their life. Even though the only connection they have to that realtor is a one-time business transaction, they choose to help the realtor because of this person's kindness and professionalism. Another example might be a person helping you when you really need it, just because they understand.

What Type of Relationship Do You Want with Yourself?

Do you respect and love yourself enough to take care of *you* first, not last? I raise this question because people often believe it's selfish to take care of their own needs first. I'm not talking about major needs such as going to work to earn an income, taking care of your children, or buying a car. I'm referring to taking time to nurture your *self*—taking proper nutritional care of yourself, exercising, and getting enough rest. Do you overwork? Overspend? Overeat? Overcommit? Over-_(fill in the blank)?

Anytime you over-engage in energy use and don't take the time to replace that energy, you are not properly nurturing yourself. You need to find a balanced approach to taking care of, regenerating, and re-energizing yourself before you can live an abundant, prosperous, stress-free life filled with peace and joy.

One of the easiest ways to remember to take care of yourself is to place at least one candle on the nightstand beside your bed. Be sure it is contained in a safe vessel to prevent accidents. Three times a week, take a few minutes just for you. Retreat to your bedroom, light your candle, and play some nurturing music. Spend at least fifteen minutes in this quiet space to allow your mind and soul to reach complete calm and peace. Then, and only then, will you begin to re- energize and nurture yourself. Be sure to remind family members that you are not to be disturbed during those fifteen minutes of peace and quiet; fifteen minutes is surely not too much to ask.

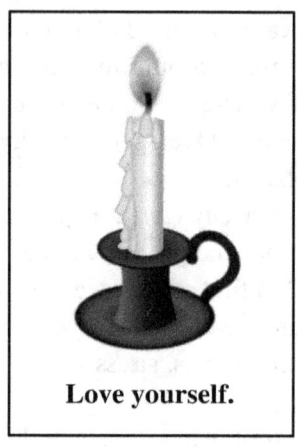

Love yourself.

Additionally, place something beautiful—something that reminds you of how special you really are—in the southwest corner of your bedroom (refer to your Shape of Life Map to locate this area). This might be a gorgeous bouquet of silk flowers in bright or soft earth tones, a picture of you at a happy time in your life, a picture of you surrounded by family members or friends, or even a collection of something you love. If you use the picture suggestion, be sure the frame is an earth-tone color, made of glass or ceramic.

You need to build this type of respectful and loving relationship with yourself before you concentrate on creating successful relationships with others. If you don't love and respect yourself, why would you expect others to? Remember, there is no other human being in the entire world exactly like you. Love and respect *you* first.

What Kind of Personal Relationships Do You Want with Others?

What kind of "relationship energy" are you looking for? How do you shift the negative energy if the relationship is not what you want or not in your best interest? Realize that there is a major difference between a relationship you want and one that is in your best interest—select carefully. Some relationships should be terminated if they are harmful to you or are significant energy-drainers.

In the Adult-to-Adult scenario, you may have a family member or friend who is always filled with negative energy and negative news. You may try to avoid this person because every conversation or encounter with them drains you. This relationship may even be an unequal relationship of convenience (theirs, not yours). Do you really want that type of person in your world permanently?

In healthy, positive-energy relationships, each friend or partner gives positive energy equally to the other. If that's not the case in some of your relationships, you may want to consider ending your involvement with them along with their negative energy or, at a minimum, limiting your contact with them. That's why it is so important to evaluate potential long-term relationships in the prism of equal energy. It's easy to start a long-term relationship or a marriage but much more difficult to end an unfulfilling, unequal, energy-draining relationship.

If any of your relationships with friends or family members are unsatisfying, then it's time to shift those negative energy relationships to positive. Begin by uncluttering the two most significant relationship areas of your home—the southwest and the east area of your family/living room. Remember to use the Shape of Life Map to locate the correct areas of your home. If the relationship in question is an intimate one with a significant other or a spouse, then unclutter those same areas along with the southwest area in your bedroom.

Once those areas are uncluttered, energize them. In the southwest area, place something that symbolizes a healthy, equal relationship for you, such as a collection of your favorite things or pictures of family or friends who represent the kind of relationships you'd like to have. You can also use a bouquet of flowers. One flower represents you and each of the other flowers symbolizes a relationship of your choice, or the entire bouquet can symbolize a wide variety of equal but different relationships. If the relationship is intimate, such as a spouse, use the same process in your bedroom but think pairs, couples, or togetherness for your southwest area enhancement. A bud vase with two flowers of equal size, a picture of two Adirondack chairs on the beach, or a painting of two hearts intertwined would all work well. This is a great opportunity to use your creativity to suit your personal taste.

In the east area, place a healthy, upward-reaching green plant; silk will work if you don't have a green thumb or the right amount of light. The plant energizes new beginnings, giving birth to new relationships, and changing existing ones for the better. This process will create positive energy for current and future relationships as well as shift existing negative-energy relationships into either neutral or positive. Be aware, though, that life-changes such as this don't happen overnight. It often takes time for energy to make this kind of positive shift permanent.

If you're an adult who is recovering from a bad relationship experience during your childhood, take a break by going for a long walk on the beach or in the park. Open yourself up to allow new energy and new thinking to enter.

Being outside will help clear your thinking, force you to breathe fresh air, and provide you a warm ray of sunshine that will allow you to look at life differently. It's not always easy to make major changes in your life, but it does take a willingness to allow new energy to enter your world so change can happen.

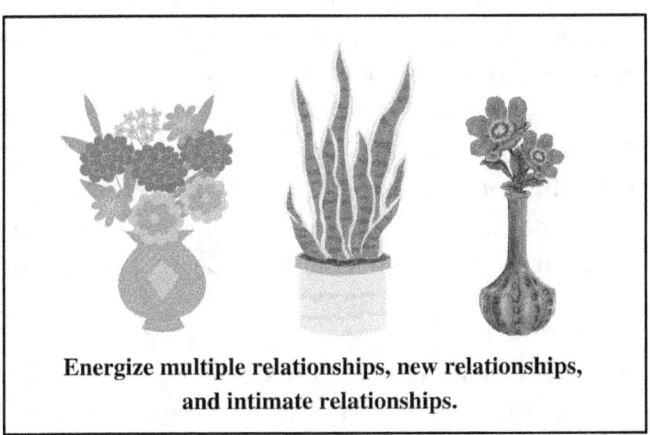

Energize multiple relationships, new relationships, and intimate relationships.

Healthy Parent/Child Relationships

When the parent/child relationship is balanced, the parent is a leader, teacher, supervisor, and benevolent ruler all at once. A parent has the responsibility of raising a child to become an independent, contributing adult to society, and a child has the responsibility of learning how to become such an adult.

The parent should always be the one in control until the child reaches an age of maturity where they can handle increasing amounts of responsibility and independence. The tendency in our society is to be less of a parent the older the child gets. The truth, however, is that a pre-teen or teen needs parenting more and in different ways to keep them on course.

Even a young adult child still needs parenting. It may be a different type of parenting, but it's still parenting.

Positive Energy Parenting Guidelines

- Establish family values at the birth of your first child and maintain them even after the child leaves home.
- Establish family rules in the beginning but make them flexible enough to allow for the individuality and the growing maturity of the child.
- Establish moral values on day one and maintain them your entire life. Be an example for your children to follow.
- If you do the above three points unwaveringly, always expect respect from your children. Do not allow anything less.

When you chose to bring a new life into the world, you also chose to become a full-time parent. The two are inseparable. Not every adult needs to be a parent, but every child needs and wants parents and a secure nurturing family environment. That is the ideal parent/child energy relationship. You can use the same types of relationship energy enhancements discussed earlier to energize your parent/child relationships. Make sure you use child-appropriate symbols, such as happy pictures with your child or a statue of a nurturing mother animal with its offspring. Place your enhancements in the family room and perhaps in the child's bedroom as well. We'll review more about children in the If Your Child's Walls Could Talk chapter.

Positive energy serves the child and parent well.

Business and Professional Relationships

Usually, business and professional relationships are ones that are mandated because you don't always get to choose your workmates or customers/clients. The challenge here is that you might have to spend a great deal of time with these people so you need to ensure that, at a minimum, they're not energy drainers.

Even though you may be able to avoid some of these people some of the time, you often can't count on that as a solution. You need to take a more proactive to either neutralize negative energy or convert the energy from business and professional relationships into something positive and supportive.

First, adopt the outlook that you are in a hassle-free, productive environment and that your goal is to be part of a team that is results-oriented. This outlook removes a competitive, "one-upmanship" attitude and puts you into the "good teammate" category.

Second, arrange your work space so you have at least a partial view of the door. This is a position of power and control. The worst energy position is to have your back to the door or the entrance to your work area. This position provides negative, stress-producing, "stab you in the back" kind of energy. If you can't avoid such an arrangement, place a mirror or something shiny on your desk so you can always see people approaching from behind. We will cover how to create a successful and positive energy workplace environment in more detail in the From Clutter and Stress to Workplace Success chapter.

Third, you can energize relationships with your co-workers and boss by placing something that symbolizes teamwork energy in the southwest corner of your work space. For example, you could use a teamwork poster, a picture of your favorite sports team, or a photo of you and your boss and peers celebrating the successful completion of a major project. Be sure to unclutter this area first or you'll be energizing the chaos and clutter as well as negatively energizing working relationships with co-workers.

A clutter-free desk positioned so you can see the entrance at all times provides the best energy for success.

Helpful People Relationships

Helpful people are those who help you accomplish your goals and objectives, both personal and professional. A helpful person could be a mentor, a parent, a friend, a spouse, a neighbor, a co-worker, or even a stranger.

In order to stimulate "helpful people" positive energy, you need to look to the northwest corner of your family room or workplace. Again, remove any clutter first. One of the easiest ways to energize this area is to make a picture collage of those who have been of great or unexpected help to you in the past. Another option, for example, would be a photo of Lance Armstrong and the Tour de France bicycling team. They represent the ultimate in co-workers supporting each other—in other words, helpful people. Motivational posters work well too.

Frame the pictures in silver, as that is the energy element representing the northwest. Use only four or five pictures and be selective. If you can't recall a helpful person or don't have any pictures, display something in silver, like a trophy or a round silver vase.

Create Balanced Relationship Energy

It doesn't matter if you're developing a new relationship, repairing an existing one, or renewing an old one, the process is the same. Relationships, whether personal or professional, are all about energy—both the energy you give to or take from them and the energy they take or give to you.

To improve or repair a relationship with positive energy, just follow the guidelines laid out in this section for the various types of relationships. To recap, first ensure there is no clutter, and then use positive energy to create the types of relationships you'd like to have. This is a great chance to exercise your imagination...*let it run free!*

We sometimes get so wrapped up in bad news and negative energy that we must constantly be on guard and find new, uplifting ways to re-energize ourselves. One of the best ways to do this is to create meaningful, positively energized, equal relationships.

Now it's time to turn inward, toward the relationship you have with yourself. Let's eliminate negative thinking, regenerate and store positive energy, and create an Intentions Board to accomplish your goals.

Chapter 7

A New You—Imagine It Now!

This chapter is all about you. Now that you've learned some of the basics about balancing and energizing your surroundings, it's time to create your own personal nurturing energy plan.

Do you ever find yourself playing mind-numbing games? Do you ever catch yourself staring out a window, only to finally "come to"? Have you ever watched hours of television or driven for miles and not really remembered what you saw?

Many people experience such events occasionally. But when these things occur on a regular basis, your body and mind are trying to tell you something: *You are running low on energy!* You can go for days, weeks, or even years without re-energizing, but eventually your body will scream, *"Stop and pay attention to me!"*

What your body yearns for is complete quiet and rest—no telephones, no television, no electronic games, no internet. Just rest. For your body to regenerate and re-energize itself, it must have balance to combat all the things that bombarded it daily. Your body does this by complete, unadulterated rest. Your body will demand sleep—more sleep than you are accustomed to getting. A quiet peace-filled home becomes a sanctuary where both the soul and the body will regenerate.

It's All about You

One of the tenets of Feng Shu is to live life to the fullest. Think about your own life. When was the last time you took a long, hot shower or bubble bath? When was the last time you lit a candle while listening to peaceful music? When was the last time you curled up with a great book and spent the entire day just reading? When was the last time you walked in the rain, stopped to look at a daisy, watched a butterfly float lazily through the sky, or observed in amazement a hummingbird moving its wings at an average of seventy to eighty beats per second while hovering endlessly in mid-air gathering nectar? When was the last time you just sat on the beach and daydreamed while listening to the waves kiss the shore? It is during these moments that you will find peace within and connection with your higher self. When was the last time you took time for you?

If you haven't done at least one of the above (or something similar) in the past week, then this chapter is for you. You received the gift of life when you were born. Unfortunately, it's a gift that most people never even think about until they're so old that they no longer have the energy, health, or desire to make changes.

But this precious gift impacts each of us dramatically. Yet we rarely have or take time to think about life…to think about why we're here now. Are we here to do something special? Or are we here to grow up into productive adults, raise a family, get a job, spoil grandchildren, or go to meetings and luncheons? Somewhere along the way, you may start wondering, "Is this all there is? Is this all life is about?"

How are you taking care of this gift, your life? Are you running low on energy? Is your body shouting at you to pay attention? Is your "tide out"? When your "tide is out," your depleted energy makes it near impossible to stay focused and to concentrate. It's your body's way of telling you that you need to rest and allow it and your mind to re-energize. The more you ignore your "tide is out" symptoms, the further out your tide will go…eventually forcing you to recognize that something could be going seriously wrong.

For a writer, a "tide is out" symptom would be writer's block. For an artist, it would take the form of thinking, "I can't paint; I don't know what to paint; my painting looks awful." For others, a "tide out" symptom may take the form of getting sick too often, pulling a tendon, never quite feeling well, or having things always go wrong. These are all symptoms of your tide being out and your body telling you to take notice and listen to its cry for help.

If you think you can wait out these symptoms and return to normal, think again. You can't. Your body won't allow that to happen. Even if you do not recognize the need to care for your physical, mental, and spiritual self, your body does. Think about it. You take good care of your automobile—you fuel it, you change its oil, lubricate its joints, give it a checkup every 20,000 miles, and put new tires on it as needed. Do you pay that much attention to caring for you? Yes, many people go to gyms to work out or walk every day, but that's just not the same as taking care of you. Such activities are left-brained thinking and lead to physical activity that helps keep your body in shape and your mind tense. Of course, physical activity is important. But to rest, restore, and revitalize you need right-brain creativity, thinking, and activities like reading, meditation, painting, writing, sculpting, and listening to music.

When your body is exhausted, you have no choice but to make time to rest and repair both your health and your energy. If you don't create time to regenerate your energy, your body will find ways to force you to do so. Whether you are leaking small or large amounts of energy, to "repair" yourself, you need to take a one-hour re-energizing break every week for at least six weeks.

Here are just a few ways to use that one-hour break to regenerate your energy:

- Pamper your body with a quiet massage, pedicure, facial, or the like.
- Go to a park or beach; sit and listen to the birds sing.
- Sit on your porch or lanai and watch the clouds float by.
- Sit in your favorite chair and quietly pet your dog or cat.
- Do nothing in your favorite spot.

The important thing here is to *do nothing*. Let your mind and body slip into a complete rest mode for at least one hour a week for six weeks. Would it be helpful if you could do nothing for more than one hour at a time or more often than once a week? Absolutely. Could you do it longer than six weeks? Yes. But six weeks is the minimum amount of rest a person needs to re-energize enough to be able to fully concentrate again and focus on those things that matter in their world. After the six-week regenerating process, re-energize by spending at least one hour doing nothing, at least once a month.

Regenerate your energy regularly to prevent your "tide going out."

Reflect So You Can Unclutter

You need new positive energy to create positive change in your life. Holding onto old ways of doing things that may not be working creates negative energy, which results in stagnation and many unresolved issues or unfinished projects. Some symptoms of such energy stagnation are relationships that aren't what you want, jobs that don't turn out the way you had hoped, not getting that promotion or pay raise you were promised, and even a constant, nagging feeling that you are never in the right place at the right time.

To shift your energy, begin by taking a close look at *what you have*, because it's a mirror-reflection of who you are and the choices you've made. Review your life to see if you're the same person today that you were just a few years ago. As you look back, think about the decisions and changes you've made that have led you to the present. Are you better off today than you were five years ago? Look at the things and people in your surroundings then and now. Do you have a better outlook on life today? If yes, what did you do to accomplish that positive change? Did you change relationships, jobs, homes, or attitudes? If your outlook today is not better, reflect on where you are today and why.

Since Feng Shui is all about using positive energy to bring about desired results, you need to determine what parts of your past were filled with good energy. Those are the thoughts and memories you want to keep. Equally important is to determine what parts of your past were filled with negative energy and eliminate those from your life.

The best way to do this is to make two columns on a notepad. Label the left column "negative" and the right column "positive." In the left column, write everything in your memories and your surroundings that does not provide you positive energy. In the right column, write only positive energy and supportive thoughts and things. The rule of thumb in Feng Shui is:

Surround yourself with only positive energy things, people, and thoughts to live a balanced, abundant life.

Therefore, if your thoughts, things, and relationships aren't providing you positive energy—or at least neutral energy—then they are sending you negative energy and you should get rid of them.

As you create your lists, write down everything you can think of, even if it seems minor or incidental. Once you've completed your list, review it with great scrutiny. Then determine if you can remove from your life those things, thoughts, and memories on your negative list. Perhaps you've already gone through this step and eliminated all the physical clutter and things in your world that are negative-energy generators. If so, that's great news! Realize, though, that relationships, thoughts, and memories are much more complex. They take more time and care to determine if or when you should get rid of them.

For example, if wellness, or lack of it, has been a long-standing issue for you, perhaps you need to look at the nutritional and exercise aspects of your life in order to shift to positive wellness-energy. Likewise, if you're no longer content with your career path or your quality of life, maybe it's time to move to a new city, so you can generate wonderful new energy, relationships, and career options in a new location. Think big and let expansive energy take hold. Don't let the borders of your mind fence you in. Moving to another location may not simply mean moving across town. In some cases, to shift energy if you're a Northerner, you may need to move south. A Midwesterner may need to move to the West Coast, and a West-Coaster may need to move east.

Use your notepad as your road map to your newly energized future. The act of putting everything down on paper will initiate the positive-energy shifting process. But don't stop there. Take action based on the information you've gleaned through observing your past and the mirror-reflection of your current life. That, plus the information on your notepad, is your road map to your positively energized, balanced, and abundant future.

Think big to allow positive energy to give you new direction for your improved future.

Feng Shui Your Thinking

Now that you're taking care of you and have uncluttered your memory, it's time to Feng Shui your thinking. What happens in your world involves not only your surroundings, but also your thoughts. Your thoughts and self-talk, as well as your surroundings, create negative energy. Once you control your surroundings as well as your thoughts, you'll be able to make positive changes in your life. The question is, "How do you change your thinking?"

When it comes to your physical surroundings, you can observe everything around you and eliminate things that generate negative energy. Just as you change your physical surroundings, you can use the same process to change your thinking. Yes, it's daunting to confront your negative thinking and self-talk. But if you do so, you'll find that it's just as easy to observe your thoughts as it is your surroundings. The following formula will help you expose your negative thinking and will get you on the road to shifting your thoughts to positive thinking.

When you're ready to worry less (negative thinking), stop putting yourself down (negative self-talk), and attract more positive energy, use this short formula:

$$F + C + PE = NR$$
(Fact + Change + Positive Energy = New Result)

Write this formula down on a piece of paper as many times as you need to. Then place the formula in places that you look often, such as your bathroom mirror or refrigerator, so it can serve as a reminder that you want to change as well as how to do it.

When you catch yourself thinking or talking to yourself negatively, such as failing an exam and saying "I'm so dumb," refer to your formula immediately. The Fact is the negative circumstance—failing an exam. The Change is your acknowledgement of your desire to change the result. The PE is the use of positive energy to change your thinking—to go from "I'm so dumb" to "I am open and eager to learn new information"—so you can achieve the New Result, such as passing the exam. Continue to practice positive energy thinking about the negative circumstance as long as necessary to shift your thought-process energy.

Yes, it really can be that simple. This formula stops negative thinking in its tracks.

It doesn't matter what the Fact is. You simply need to acknowledge that you're thinking negatively, realize you want to Change your thinking about the Fact, and use Positive Energy thinking to create the New Result. As you observe your thoughts over the weeks and months ahead, you'll be amazed at the number of times you catch yourself in the negative-energy thinking and self-talk mode.

By using the formula $F + C + PE = NR$, you'll find yourself worrying much less and enjoying life much more. By using positive energy, you will bring about desired results, plus more joy and peace in your world. Remember that life is too short to constantly worry about things that might never happen. Instead, enjoy life to its fullest by using Feng Shui to worry less and to positively energize your thinking.

Storing Positive Energy

Day-to-day living often contains far too many negative-energy issues that bombard us with numerous activities and direct our focus to tense events. But do you ever take time to listen to your body and allow it to regenerate and store energy? In order to have the reserve energy needed to deal with negative issues, your body and mind need to generate more positive energy than you use up every day. The following Feng Shui techniques can help you build up positive-energy reserves that you can access at more stressful times.

1. Realize that you are in control of your world, instead of believing that outside circumstances control you. Repeat to yourself three times every morning and evening, "*I am in control of my world.*" This will increase your personal positive energy and dimmish the feelings of negative energy, such as being helpless or being a victim.
2. Listen to upbeat music that stirs the heart and soul and makes energy surge into your life. This really works (but don't listen to it if you're going to sleep soon).
3. Create a "self-energizing center." Claim a small area in a spare bedroom, your bedroom, the den, or porch. Spend time alone in this area for ten to fifteen minutes, three times per week, to regenerate your energy. Let family members know that you'll be in your "self-energizing zone" and you're not to be disturbed for those ten to fifteen minutes. While there, listen to peaceful music, read a relaxing book, meditate, stare out the window…or do absolutely nothing at all. Just let your mind and body rest.
4. Create a "Gratitude Journal" to eliminate the anxiety, stress, and negative energy you allow to creep (or jog or race) into your life. A grateful heart and mind leave no room for unwanted negative energy. Buy a journal or notebook. At the end of every day, write down at least five positive things that happened to you during the day that you are grateful for. If you can't think of anything, try

simple things, such as you woke up in the morning alive and in a comfortable bed, the sun is shining and warming your day, you have food in your refrigerator, and so on. You can write down as many things as you can think of; don't feel that you must limit them to only five. You'll be amazed at how much better you will feel within just a few days. Being grateful for even the smallest things can put a lot of issues into perspective. Make sure you date each entry, so you can see your progress.

5. Make every day count! Realize that whatever you do today, you are exchanging for a day of your life. Everything you do each day will either bring you closer to your goals or put negative energy between you and your goals. When you choose to make every day count and take care of self first, you're choosing to succeed…by moving one day closer to accomplishing your goals.

Each of these techniques works well to help you create abundant positive energy in your life. You can then go back to any one of them, especially the gratitude journal, to draw upon your positive energy from the past when you need to in the future.

> ## Three Ways to Create a Better You
>
> **1. Surround yourself with positive people and thinking** so you can attract positive energy to help you accomplish the most important items in your life. You are developing a "can do" attitude.
>
> **2. Learn to love yourself** by respecting your commitment to self-improvement. Encourage yourself by placing a vase with two beautiful silk flowers by your bed. One flower represents you, and the other flower represents that beautiful, special person inside who deserves to be loved, respected, nurtured, and filled with positive energy thinking.
>
> **3. You are in control**, and you deserve a better life ahead. If you want to empower yourself and achieve the goals you've committed to, you need to believe you are special, **because you are.**

Create an Intentions Board to Accomplish Goals

Goals, aspirations, and good intentions are vital to anyone's future. They are also important for maintaining positive energy in your personal environment. In the past, you may have had a clear list of goals you wanted to accomplish…so clear you knew exactly where you were going to focus your energy, time, and money. Have you achieved those goals? Is that where you are today? If not, why not?

For many people, positive energy is the missing link that connects intentions to the successful completion of goals. To energize your good intentions, use a Feng Shui tool known as an Intentions Board. It will help you bridge the gap between your intentions and successful results.

An Intentions Board is like a bulletin board or a surface where you can use push pins to attach pictures and messages. Once you've decided what you'll use to create your Intentions Board, make sure it's a dedicated surface used only to support your intentions, your goals, and your dreams. The best location for your Intentions Board is either in your bedroom, if you wish it to be private, or near the door of your home that you regularly use. You need to see your board several times every day. Ideally, place it on an east wall to further encourage positive new energy to enter your life.

For each intention/goal you would like to accomplish, find something symbolic that represents your desire and place it on your board. Here are a few examples:

- If your intention is to create more peace in your life, you could place a picture of the beach, a park bench, or a chair in front of a cozy fireplace. You could also put the number "15," representing the minutes of quiet time you need at least once a week.
- To improve your health, put a picture of a sumptuous meal filled with only healthy, fresh food.
- A picture of a single candle burning will serve you well in energizing your spiritual self.
- A family-gathering picture would provide you supportive relationship energy if you are working on improving relationships.

Intentions Board Helps Accomplish Goals

Energize your goals by creating an Intentions Board
- **Spend more time together as a family**
- **Earn a better income (be specific)**
- **Take better care of me**

Using your Intentions Board is simple. You can put as many symbols and pictures on it as you feel are necessary to help you shift stagnant energy to positive success energy. If your goal has multiple levels, such as losing twenty-five pounds, you can do it in stages, thereby energizing each stage. For example, you can put the number for the next size down of clothing you'd like to wear on your board. Once you achieve that goal, move down another size-number until you reach your final goal. Using interim steps is a way to encourage yourself because you can see progress.

Remember that intentions are just intentions until you energize them and act upon them. The best intentions and goals in the world, if not acted upon, become stagnant, wasted energy. An Intentions Board, with appropriate goal-oriented symbols, creates a positive energy flow that helps you achieve your desires and intentions.

Create Your Best Life Now

Taking care of *you* is good Feng Shui. In today's world, it's easy to unbalance your body and deplete its energy. Fortunately, you can reverse the process by using some of these basic Feng Shui methods on yourself as well as your surroundings. Of course, doing so requires a deliberate plan and *action* on your part to create a successful completion. Since you're given only one body in which to live, you need to take good care of it. After all, if you don't, who will?

When you improve yourself physically and mentally, you also improve the energy in your surroundings. And that, in turn, attracts better things to your personal world. Remember the following ...

Feng Shui is the use of positive energy in your surroundings to bring about desired results.

In this case, the result is an improved, new you and a better life...a life where you are in control. Next, you will learn how clothes can energize you, make you confident and successful, and help you achieve an upbeat outlook on life.

Chapter 8

What You Wear Matters

Does your wardrobe support you in everything you do? Do you feel great no matter what you're wearing? Or does your wardrobe need an energy lift? Are you tired of wearing the same few items time and again? Is your closet full of clothes, yet you feel like you have nothing to wear? This is a challenge many people deal with as the seasons change (and perhaps the waistline as well) and it affects men and women alike.

Whether your plans for the day are in the boardroom or sitting on the deck reading a book, dressing appropriately for the energy needed for the day will make your day more productive and enjoyable. The clothes you wear, and their colors, can make a huge difference in how you accomplish the tasks ahead.

Energy is in everything and everywhere, including the clothes on your back. You can easily ensure that you have the best energy possible surrounding you as you leave home to embark on your busy day ahead. The next time you go to your closet and reach for something to wear, give some thought to what you want to accomplish that day. Then look for the colors and designs that will give you the best supportive energy. Try it…it really works!

Does Your Wardrobe Support You?

Feng Shui's positive energy principles apply to everything in your surroundings, including your clothes. Why wear something that's draping you with negative energy when you can easily shift your wardrobe to only those garments and accessories that energize you and lift your spirits? Remember this simple rule when determining whether you should purchase or wear various articles of clothing:

If something doesn't fit you, look great on you, and make you feel like a million dollars, don't buy it. If that unflattering item is already in your closet, don't wear it; get rid of it.

Following this simple rule will provide you positive, uplifting energy. If your clothing doesn't give you great personal energy, it's time to shift the energy in your closet to the positive, supportive energy you deserve in your wardrobe…and need to prosper.

Think about how you acquire your clothing and accessories. Are the different "post-holiday and seasonal sales" your way to stock up on a new wardrobe? Do you receive clothes and accessories as gifts that you may not like or that don't fit you well? Do all the sale racks lure you into the stores, instilling you with the thought, "I can buy twice as many clothes at half the price. What a deal!" Or are some of the sale items so tempting that you simply justify the purchase by thinking, "I'm sure I must have something at home that matches this."

Once you get those new clothing items home, is there room in your closet and dresser for them? Or is your closet already bulging at the seams? Have you even taken over another closet in your home? And what about all those shoes, belts, ties, and scarves scattered everywhere? Do you really need two more pairs of the exact same sneakers, four pairs of golf shoes or two pairs of purple heels, just because they're on sale? And finally, does that new item you bought really match something currently in your closet?

In order to maintain balance in your home and your life, you need to remember that everything you surround yourself with provides you with positive or negative energy—including the clothes you hang in your closet. Clothes that don't fit well, do not match, or do not make you feel good when you put them on don't belong in your closet. Not only are they causing clutter, but they are also generating stagnant negative energy. Only clothes that make you look and feel great should be in your wardrobe. No matter how much a piece of clothing is marked down on the sale rack, if it doesn't give you great energy, it shouldn't go home with you.

Purchasing a garment just because it's on sale is not a bargain if it hangs in your closet, just taking up space and collecting dust, because it doesn't match anything or because the color looked awful once you got it home. The same applies to shoes, belts, handbags, ties, scarves, shawls, and wraps. You need to know exactly what you're going to do with the items before you bring them home. And you need to decide whether they give you enough positive energy to deserve being part of your wardrobe.

When bargain shopping, buy a complete outfit or take along the piece you are trying to match.

An Energized Wardrobe Energizes You

The concept of clothing providing you something other than privacy and warmth may be a bit new to you. But in the world of Feng Shui, clothing is simply another piece of your personal environment that surrounds you daily and provides either positive, helpful energy or negative, draining energy. The things you surround yourself with, whether home furnishings, office equipment, automobiles, people, or clothing, all provide you either positive or negative energy.

Think about how you feel and look when you dress to go out on a first date, to a holiday party, or to an upscale restaurant. Do you feel upbeat, excited, self-assured, and in control? Alternatively, consider how you dress, look, and feel when you go on a job interview. Are you confident, positive, and enthusiastic? In each case, you take great care determining what you should wear and how it will impact those in your presence. But do you ever consider how your clothes impact you and your personal energy *all the time*? The colors, textures, and design of your clothing, and the way it fits, can make you feel confident and in control or weak and unimportant.

Whether your professional or personal daytime activities require a certain type of clothing or you simply prefer a certain "look," your clothing choices affect your energy. What you put on in the morning sets the tone and energy level for the day. It's no accident that you might pull out a predominantly blue outfit to wear on days that you feel down or "blue." Likewise, on days when you need to make a great impression or be "on," you might choose a red necktie or red dress, which is positive, high-energy clothing.

Color provides great supportive energy—if it's in alignment with your needs for the day. For example, you wouldn't want to wear a drab brown suit with a light tan shirt and a light-colored tie for a job interview…unless you did *not* want the job and *did* want to melt into the woodwork. You could, however, wear that same brown suit with a cream or peach-colored shirt and a medium to bright orange tie to give it that energy spark, make you look distinctive, and give you a much-needed energy edge and confidence boost.

Here's another example: If you go to a social gathering wearing khakis and muted earth-tone colors, you're likely to feel low energy and possibly go unnoticed. Since those colors are neutral energy, they allow you to blend into the background. The same happens if you wear soft pastels. In addition, if the pastel is low-energy, such as soft pink, you will not only blend into the background but you will also feel as though you have no control over events surrounding you. On the other hand, bright hot pink in a shirt, blouse, or necktie will energize you…and get you noticed.

By surrounding yourself with soothing, calming colors on hectic days and energetic, uplifting colors on dreary days, you will notice an incredible difference in your attitude, your self-confidence, and the way you feel at the end of the day. Remember, for the best Feng Shui energy, surround yourself with only those things that fit well, look great on you, and make you feel like a million dollars when wearing them.

Whatever your style is, your clothes should fit well, look great on you, and make you feel like a million dollars.

Begin with Your Existing Wardrobe

Before you go on a shopping spree, scrutinize your existing wardrobe. Start by uncluttering closets and drawers to get rid of the energy-drainers and make room for those wonderful new things that will provide you with great positive energy.

- Do you have some items (other than special-occasion attire) that you seldom or never wear? If so, get rid of them or buy something that matches so you can wear

them. They're not providing you good energy by just hanging there.
- Next, try on all those things you'd like to wear but don't. If they don't look great on you or do not fit, it's time for them to go (unless you are actively working on a goal to lose weight or work out so they will look great on you).
- Finally, examine each of the garments you regularly wear to make sure they are still in good condition, they match, they look great on you…and they make you feel great.

Once you've uncluttered your closet, what remains will be a wardrobe that serves you well and provides you great positive energy for work, play, and romance.

Create Energy to Match Your Day

If you get up in the morning and grab the first thing you see in your closet, you are essentially planning to have a similar day—unplanned, un-energized, and unfocused. If you put your outfit together quickly because you're running late, you will likely find yourself similarly behind and unorganized throughout the day. Glitches, setbacks, and obstacles often happen in your closet, before the day even begins.

Commit to deciding either the night before or when you first wake up what type of day you want to have, and then dress accordingly. It's that simple. What you surround yourself with all day (in this case, your clothing) will determine your energy for the day.

Since you have already uncluttered your closet, everything remaining in it will give you supportive energy. But is it the best supportive energy for your specific activities on that day? Not only do you want to make sure you feel great and look terrific in what you wear, you also need to make sure it's providing you with the right supportive and uplifting energy you need to have the kind of day you desire.

Therefore, determine which clothes give you lots of energy for a busy day and which are low-key and low energy for quiet, laid-back days. Take into consideration the style and color of the clothing when making this decision. Each color provides you very specific energy. The intensity (bright vs. dull) of the color also matters. For example, pastel colors provide soft, even feminine energy, while bold colors exude strong, almost aggressive energy. If you know your day will be hectic, wear bolder colored clothing with a structured fit to give you that much-needed self-control and boost of energy. If you want a laid-back day with friends and family, wear loose-fitting clothes in pastel or neutral, low-energy colors. The following list of colors and their energy meaning can help you determine what might work best for your day ahead.

Red	Energetic and bold, self-confident
Yellow	Optimistic, a little goes a long way
Blue	Calm and in control to cold and distant
Orange	Uplifting, has pizzazz
Green	Fresh and productive
Purple	Inspiring and regal
Pink	Calm but without power
Indigo	Knowledgable
Brown	Down-to-earth, dependable, and productive
Black	All-encompassing energy, strength to overpowering
White	Purity, crisp and clean

When it comes to clothing, energy comes in all sizes, shapes, patterns, and colors. And, as you can see, colors come in a variety of energy values as well. If you have a favorite suit that's somewhat subdued and low-energy but you love to wear it because you feel great in it, you can use accessories to give it some pizzazz…and give you that much-needed energy boost. Take a lesson from newscast anchors. The men wear bright—and sometimes shocking—neckties, while women wear distinct jewelry and colorful jackets. They obviously understand the use of color energy and what it takes to be noticed.

Accessories Provide You an Energy Boost

The Right Energy for the Job

Try following a few basic Feng Shui guidelines on how to energize yourself by choosing the right energy clothes for the day or event ahead.

- Wear neutral colors on days you want to accomplish a lot with minimum interruptions.
- Wear bright colors on days you need to be very productive, upbeat, and on the go all day.
- Wear fitted clothes in darker colors on days when you need to be in total self-control.

- Wear loose-fitting, light-colored clothes on days when you wish to work at a more leisurely pace or to relax.
- Wear black when you want to absorb all the energy of the moment or utilize that energy to make a statement.
- Wear red when you want to be confident and secure in who you are or when you want to be noticed.

Start noticing how you feel when you're wearing certain colors and designs. Pay attention to how your day goes while wearing them. Do you feel drained at the end of the day? Or do you still have enough energy left to enjoy your evening with your family or friends?

Every day, evaluate the clothes you're wearing to determine if they're providing you the energy you need. Perhaps that great pair of khakis needs to be energized by adding a brighter shirt or colorful scarf or necktie. If you wish to wear a brightly colored dress but feel its energy may be too much for the occasion, tone it down with an appropriate neutral-colored jacket.

Consider your undergarments and shoes too. For undergarments, fit and comfort win over any other energy consideration. From an energy perspective, how it looks on you and how you feel wearing it are less important than comfort.

When evaluating your shoe wardrobe, give attention to safety first. Feng Shui is not only about the use of positive energy but also about safety. Shoes should look good, feel comfortable when wearing them, and be safe to walk in. When buying new shoes, be sure to consider fit, comfort, *and safety*.

Shop with Energy in Mind

With your new knowledge, you can now shop all the sales racks with energy as part of the criteria so you will purchase only those garments and accessories that give you positive, supportive energy. Judge your new purchases as follows:

- Do you like the material and how it feels to the touch?
- Do you like the way you feel when you try the garment on?
- Do you like the way you look when wearing the garment?
- Does the color of the garment give you an energy lift or does it leave you feeling down?
- Does it need another piece to complete the outfit? If yes, buy it at the same time so you have a good match and can wear it immediately.
- Determine how you're going to use the garment before you buy it. Only then will you know if it will provide you the appropriate energy.
- Once you get it home, if it has multiple pieces, hang all the pieces together so they are available as a complete outfit at a moment's notice.

If you love the material, the design, and the way you feel and look in the garment, and it gives you a lift, then the energy is positive for you and it will be a wise addition to your wardrobe. If you have any hesitation as to whether it looks great on you or whether you love it, *do not buy it!* It will not provide you that great positive energy you want and need surrounding you.

Energized Wardrobes Really Work

Feng Shui is the use of positive energy in your life and surroundings, including your wardrobe, to bring about desired results. In this case, the desired result is a more confident, self-assured and in-control you, which leads to a more successful and enjoyable life. By using energy as one of the criteria for your clothing purchases (or for removing clothes from your wardrobe), you eliminate emotion-driven impulse decisions. And you stop holding onto clothes that do not serve you well.

Follow the same energy-elimination and purchasing procedures for your shoes, accessories, scarves, ties, purses, vests, coats, and jewelry. Accessories are an important part of your wardrobe because that is where you can put the brightest colors and most noticeable shapes. They are what create "your style" and that little something extra called *panache*.

Chapter 9

If Your Child's Walls Could Talk, What Would You Learn?

Many parents today spend thousands of dollars on tutors, special classes, and therapists in their quest to get their child to sleep, behave, or study. What they may not realize, though, is that their child's physical environment affects their behavior. Negative energy in the nursery or a child's room may lead to unhealthy sleeping habits, aggressive behavior, poor grades, and less than desirable parent/child and teacher/child relationships.

The color of a child's bedroom, the pictures on the walls and the placement of the bed all provide either positive, supportive energy or negative energy. For example, the posters on their walls are the last thing they see when going to bed at night and the first thing they see when getting up. Are their posters calming, reassuring, peaceful, and filled with positive messages? Or do they contain a scary, belligerent, or aggressive message? Are those posters and pictures sending the message you want your child to receive?

Does Feng Shui Work for Children Too?

You *can* shift the energy of a child's bedroom from loud, bold, and rebellious to peaceful, happy, and harmonious. Because energy knows no age boundaries, Feng Shui works as well for children and adolescents as it does for adults. In fact, in ancient China, emperors believed they could "change their destiny" through the proper use of Feng Shui. And great abundance was evident in the longevity of their seniors and large families filled with many children.

Will using Feng Shui to balance the home make a difference in your child's life? Does Feng Shui really work in the nursery? Can you use Feng Shui to encourage children to study and or follow the family rules?

The answer is a resounding "Yes"! Whether you are a parent, grandparent, or guardian, Feng Shui and its principles of positive energy will make a huge difference in everyone's life, especially young and impressionable children. What you surround your children with—the colors on the walls, the pictures and posters they look at every day, and the music they hear—all have a profound impact on their thoughts, values, and actions. Much is written these days about nourishing children's bodies. But little is written about nurturing their hearts and souls so they can become productive, well-balanced adults who contribute positively to society.

Color Energy Makes a Difference

What color are the walls in your children's bedrooms? Are they peaceful colors that encourage quiet, rest, concentration, and study? Or are they bright colors that encourage activity, stir up energy, and stimulate the mind so it's in constant motion? The colors you surround a child with in their personal space will make a huge difference in their attitude and well-being. The impact can be enormous.

It doesn't matter how old your child is, the bedroom should be a place of peace and calm. As the walls provide a large amount of energy in the room because of their size, you can start to create a calm atmosphere by using soothing colors on the walls. Use light pastel shades but let the child choose the actual color. However (and you may be surprised to hear this), don't use white. In a child's room, white is a harsh, high-energy color that discourages quiet and rest and doesn't appeal to the gentler side of a child's personality. The ideal colors can range from a variety of soft greens and blues to soft pinks and lavenders.

Paint walls soft colors to provide calm and peaceful energy.

The key to using color effectively in a child's bedroom is to ensure that there is just a blush of color, making it pastel, as noted in the Peaceful Color Palette for Children chart. You can add pops of color through pictures and posters on the walls. Make sure wall décor is happy and upbeat or inspiring

Peaceful Color Palette for Children

Color	Energy Type	Traits/Uses
Pink, Light Lavender	Calm	Associated with sweetness and innocence; most used color for candy, girls' bedrooms, and clothing; used in prison cells to calm prisoners
Cream, Soft Yellow	Optimism	Least popular hue in the color spectrum when bright; stimulates memory, nervous system, and internal organs; associated with high-pitched sounds, sour smells, heat, and triangles; babies cry more in yellow rooms—use only cream on children's walls
Soft Blue, Blue Violet	Calm	Non-threatening and neutral; color of trust, longevity, and dependability; induces calming effect; lowers blood pressure; restful, calming, strengthens immune and nervous systems; increases sense of security for children
Peach, Light Salmon	Uplifting	Brightest color in the spectrum; use peach or flesh tones on walls; use sparingly unless toned down; associated with earth tones and grounding; encourages joy and happiness; youthful color that pleases the inner child
Light Mint, Sage, Celery Green	New	Evokes a sense of relaxation, comfort, and quietness; easiest color for the eye to see; most restful; associated with spring, new growth, and new beginnings; holding rooms in theaters and studios are painted green to lower anxiety; reflects love, harmony, peace, and goodwill toward others; provides mental and physical equilibrium; great for stress

Infants and Preschoolers

Let's begin at the beginning—the nursery. The primary function of a nursery is to create a peaceful and safe setting for the child to sleep; therefore, that's the first energy principle to apply. Infants need a lot of rest so their bodies can grow and their minds can develop. They also need a place where they can learn the household rules, develop good sleeping habits, relate to their new world, and visually explore their surroundings. In order to create this much-needed peaceful setting, the nursery room colors should be pastel. Any patterns used should have a gentle, flowing movement with few sharp edges. Use no primary colors here.

To expose the infant to the full spectrum of colors, include a pastel version of the color wheel in the nursery. A large, gently arching pastel rainbow wall art would be a good example. Some parents have painted a soft rainbow mural on a complete wall. You can incorporate other colors in the form of pictures, linens, and even hanging toys over a crib. Continue to add to the full spectrum of colors as the child grows older but maintain the pastel values to retain peace and calm. Overstimulation with bright colors and many shapes in the nursery will cause anxiety and restlessness in the infant.

Ideally, the bedroom should provide a place for only two activities for infants and young children. First, the bedroom should be a place for genuine rest. Second, it should be a sanctuary from the noise and activity in the rest of the house. Infants' and young children's bodies are constantly growing, and their minds are like sponges, absorbing everything they see and hear twenty-four hours per day, seven days per week. Therefore, they need quiet space for their minds and bodies to rest and regenerate.

Remember, Feng Shui is all about the use of positive energy to bring about a desired result. In this case, the desired result is peace and calm as infants and young children develop and grow. In the case of newborns and toddlers, cuddle them in their bedrooms and surround them with peaceful nurturing energy.

At this point you may be wondering where the child should play if the bedroom is for sleep and sanctuary. The answer is to create colorful play areas away from their sleeping area, preferably in another room. Play areas should be higher energy and filled with bright colors, many shapes, different textures, and appropriate sounds to encourage activity and creativity (but not aggressive behavior and disobedience). This is where you put the primary colors. If their play area must be maintained in the bedroom, try to keep it separated from the sleeping area to avoid overstimulation and irritability.

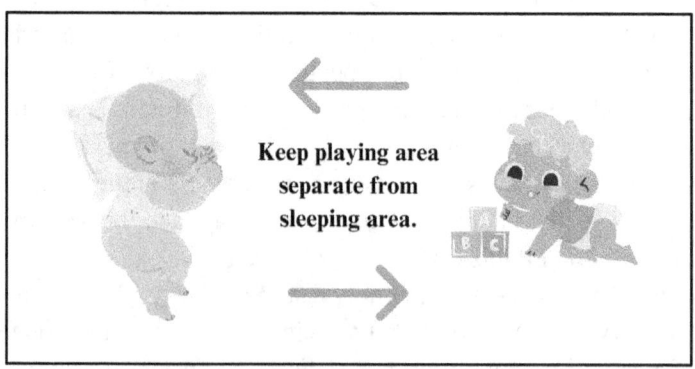

The School-Aged Child

For school-aged children (elementary or primary years), the main use for their bedroom should still be for sleep and, when appropriate, homework. Keep the wall colors pastel and use pictures, pillows, and stuffed animals to add bright color splashes to the room. Music played in the bedroom should also reflect the reason for the room— peacefulness, sleep, adherence to family values, and learning. If possible, play areas with lots of stimulation through colors, shapes and sounds should be reserved for another part of the house. If the bedroom is used for stimulating activities in addition to rest, a child's body gets confused at such an early, formative stage in life and can't decide whether they should rest in their room or remain constantly on the go.

At this stage, take another look at the wall color to make sure it's conducive to learning and resting. The best colors for that process to take place are light blue, light green, soft peach, or pastel teal. These colors are not only peaceful but also encourage learning energy.

Obtain a solid bed with a headboard as soon as the child is out of the crib. This will provide solid sleep, security, safety, and positive supportive energy. Do not allow a child to sleep on a mattress on the floor, as that creates insecure and unsafe negative energy. Position the child's bed on a solid wall farthest from the door, with no window behind the headboard or above the bed. This provides the best energy area for sleep and safety.

Place the child's desk in the northeast corner of the room to further energize knowledge and education. See the bed placement diagram in the Calm Your Chaos chapter under the Bedroom section.

Colors and visual images are powerful for a child. They affect the way the child looks at the world and interacts with parents, relatives, teachers, and friends. In fact, these images are so powerful that children will look for friends who share the same images and idols, further imbedding the negative or positive energy created by them. You can shift a child's entire outlook on life by shifting negative energy in a bedroom to upbeat, peaceful, positive energy. By changing to positive energy through the color of their walls, the pictures on their walls, and the music they listen to, you can change their lives.

When helping your child choose pictures and posters for the walls, make sure the images represent a lifestyle that you view as healthy or want your child to imitate. Also, avoid loud colors. The wrong images can be distracting and create energy not conducive to learning, respect for others, or resting. Children often try to become—sometimes unconsciously—what they last see at night when going to sleep and what they first see when waking up. Is their "want-to-be-hero" consistent with your values and what you want for your child?

If your children are in the tween years, remember that you're the one in charge. If you decide that you need to shift energy in their rooms to help them study and relate positively to you and others, do so. You'll be amazed at the positive results.

Children are dramatically influenced by their peers, their idols, and mass electronic communication. Closely monitoring these influences will help you guide them. When you create a bedroom that's a sanctuary and a place to study, it is much easier to have your child remain within the framework of the household rules as they get older. For example, if you start with the fundamental bedroom rules during infancy and early childhood, your child will recognize that these rules are for making their life more secure. And they'll not only choose to live within the family guidelines but they'll also realize the rules protect them.

Extend family rules and values to electronic equipment. Always know what your child listens to, watches, and who they talk to on the computer. Only purchase music and games you want them to hear and play. Use the V-chip and parental control blocking on all televisions. Use online child protection software and apps on all computers.

The Teen Years

A different challenge comes when a child reaches their teens. Even though teens think they want more freedom, they actually need parental guidance and rules as much now—and perhaps even more—than when they were toddlers and youngsters. If you've had the opportunity to shape their behavior, thinking, and relationship-value systems before they reach this stage using Feng Shui's positive energy principles, it will be much easier to deal with the teen years.

Just as when your child was younger, it's important for a teen's room to remain a sanctuary for rest and study, rather than a place of isolation for looking at pictures, watching TV, text messaging, internet surfing, or listening to the music of those who would lead them into a lifestyle unacceptable to you. A teen's room should also be painted in pastel colors—no bold shades. The energy of the pastels will provide them a calm setting and give you better control over their habits and attitude.

Even more important at this age, the posters and pictures on the walls and the music played in that bedroom must be consistent with the energy intent of rest, respectful relationships, and learning, as well as your family values. Are the images and lyrics peaceful? Or do they symbolize turbulence? Are they antisocial, racial, or militant? The parent's role is to make sure their children are being properly influenced by the energy in their bedrooms.

If your teen's idols are not appropriate role models, take action and change the posters to something more in alignment with your family values. Energy is a powerful thing, and the energy in the pictures and music in a teen's room can mold their thought processes and actions for years to come. What you surround them with determines their attitudes toward relationships (especially with parents), study habits, and passive or aggressive behavior.

Unclutter to Promote Creativity

Help your children to unclutter their world and organize it in ways that will encourage positive energy, which is a long-term building block for creativity. An uncluttered, organized room is conducive to studying, resting, and reinforcing a lifestyle that encourages creativity and wholesomeness. An organized room is the foundation for a successful future. Uncluttering your child's room will also give you the opportunity to teach your child to:

- Let go of things no longer needed, as they create stagnant energy.
- Give to others in need.

- Create a life lesson that links organization to success.

To help your child develop an "uncluttering" mindset, use three boxes. Label the first one "Keep," the second one "Share," and the third one "Toss." Then, engage them in the process of sorting and uncluttering their bedroom or toy closet, so they can learn values and organizational skills. Repeat this activity yearly. As your child grows, they need to be introduced to toys and activities that are challenging and age appropriate.

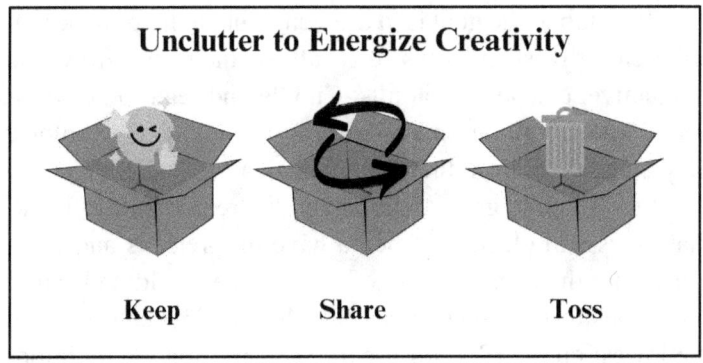

A space that is both quiet and empty is necessary for a child's inner creative self to rise to the surface. By providing a quiet, neutral background without clutter, and limiting "stuff," you energize their ability to allow their creative juices to flow.

Provide children of all ages with as many outside creative activities as possible in the creative arts—such as painting, sculpting, music, dancing, and writing—even if you have to drive miles to do so. They'll learn invaluable lessons in discipline and self-respect, while also gaining self-confidence and self-control.

Positive Energy Brings Desired Results

Use positive energy in a child's life to influence good sleep habits, family values, and positive thinking and action. It doesn't matter if the child is an infant or a teen. Feng Shui is a wonderful tool for parents, grandparents, and guardians to use when trying to positively influence a child's future.

Create a soft, soothing sanctuary in their bedroom that provides rest, security, and peaceful energy conducive to learning, living by family rules, and participating in a lifetime guided by family values.

Remember, the goal is to use Feng Shui to help shape your children's lives in ways that allow them to grow into productive, considerate adults. Cuddle and read to newborns and toddlers with peaceful, nurturing energy. Create colorful play areas away from their sleeping area.

As your child grows, remember the tremendous influence that peers and electronic media have on preteens and teens. For some, their entire view of the outside world and family life comes from those sources. Teachers and parents are often the lowest on their list for seeking out information, opinions, and guidance. Just remember—you are in charge, and if you need to shift energy in their rooms to help them study and relate positively to society, take charge and do so now.

Chapter 10

From Clutter and Stress to Workplace Success

Whether you are a stay-at-home mom, a retiree with a home office, a remote worker, a nine-to-five cubicle dweller, or someone juggling a career in the corner office and a young family, this chapter will provide you ways to organize and energize your office to minimize stress and maximize productivity.

Are you ready to introduce positive change into your workplace or office space…the kind of change that's not disruptive and doesn't create more stress? Are you looking to improve your business and productivity now, not at some undefined time in the future? By using Feng Shui methods, you can change your physical work environment in a way that will improve your productivity, reduce your stress, and make work more enjoyable and profitable.

Feng Shui is about using the physical environment of your workplace, whether it's in your home or in an office building, to create calm where there is stress and to improve focus. From a business standpoint, balance and harmony in the workplace are critical for employee retention, customer loyalty, and maintaining a competitive edge. From a personal standpoint, balance and harmony in the workplace reduces burnout, increases happiness, and makes work more enjoyable.

In order to make a positive change in your professional world, start with your surroundings. Maximize the positive energy in your physical work environment to help position you and your company for future success and an improved bottom line. The same principles would also apply, by the way, to the home office, where you may earn a living, correspond with friends, or write that novel you've been dreaming about.

You can develop an action plan that uses positive energy to create balance in your work environment so that you'll be more in control of your future, your success, and your world.

Reduce Stress—Improve Success

Have you ever said to yourself, "I'd be happier if I made more money"? Many of us have.

Or how about, "If I were more successful, my life would be so much better. I'd be less stressed and have better relationships."

The truth is, you can be happier, have better work and personal relationships, and increased prosperity if you get rid of clutter and stress and replace them with success. By implementing the three easy Feng Shui steps I'm going to teach you, you will reduce stress, improve your focus and productivity, and achieve higher levels of success!

Better concentration and focus lead to making good decisions, which is vital if you're to succeed, meet deadlines, and be more productive. We all encounter so many distractions every day. That's why we must develop the proper energy needed for maximum productivity while we're at work and the discipline to leave work behind at the end of the day. By positively shifting your work-space energy, you'll create a positive energy shift for those in your immediate surroundings, both at work and at home.

Increase Prosperity by Aligning Thoughts, Actions, and Surroundings

You're probably wondering, "How do I get rid of the negative energy and stress in my business or professional life? Can I create a positive energy shift in my workplace to be more successful?"

The answer once again is a loud "Yes." You can get rid of the stress by using the steps in this book. And yes, you can make your career more successful. By using a few basic Feng Shui principles, you can make positive changes in your life, especially regarding prosperity and income generation.

Remember, Feng Shui is the use of positive energy to bring about desired results, in this case prosperity and success. To create a positive shift in success and prosperity energy you need to align your thoughts, actions, and surroundings with your objectives. You can enhance the energy flow in the areas of your business or home office that are crucial to the positive flow of income in your life. How? The answer is simple: *Get rid of all the clutter that is taking over your office and creating negative energy, chaos, and stress.* Clutter will drain positive energy and make you disorganized, unproductive, and very, very stressed.

Just what does clutter have to do with success? Clutter creates and holds stagnant negative energy, creates a mental and physical block, and stands in the way of new energy—things that will motivate and encourage you. You can *choose* to use positive energy to de-stress your world and unclutter your surroundings.

When using positive energy and three basic Feng Shui steps, you can:

- Bring balance to a stress-filled workday
- Create harmony where there is anxiety
- Improve working relationships that are now energy-drainers
- Become more focused and productive
- Have energy left at day's end to participate in family activities and personal interests

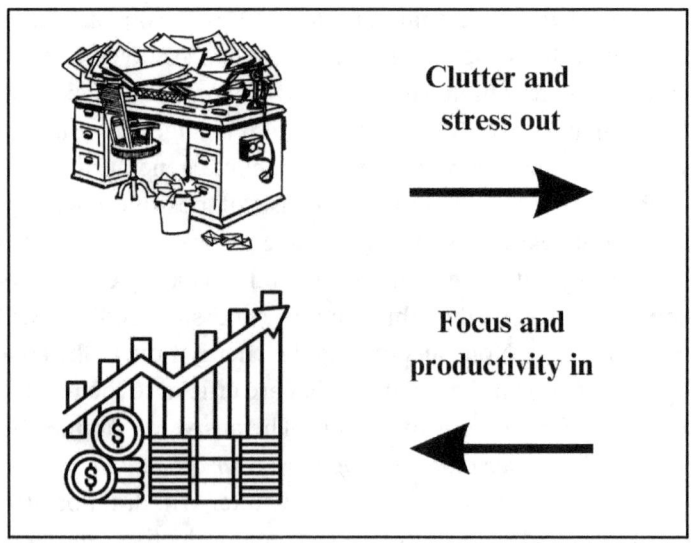

Step 1: Improve Focus by Creating a Clutter-free Zone

Clutter not only creates stagnant energy but, depending on where it's found in your office, it can also create slow or difficult areas in your life. For example, if your clutter is in the southwest area of your office, you may find your relationships with clients or co-workers waning or a bit on the difficult side. Or, if the clutter is in the center of your office, your life may seem a bit disjointed, with nothing working out the way you planned.

In general, clutter is anything you do not need, does not energize you, and has no specific purpose in your work space. Go through your desk drawers and filing cabinets. If something isn't useful, if it's outdated, if it's something you'll never read, or something no longer relevant, *get rid of it!* These same rules apply to storage areas and old filing systems. You need to eliminate clutter wherever it accumulates in order to ensure that maximum energy will flow throughout your office or work area. Some people find it easy to eliminate things that have accumulated over the weeks, months, and years. For others, the thought of such an undertaking is so overwhelming that they simply cannot begin.

Take heart though. You don't have to tackle it all at once. Instead, target only one specific area of your office; otherwise, the task will seem daunting. Take it one step at a time. Clear small sections and make sure you take it to completion. You'll see progress and feel the energy shifting…and that will be very motivating. If there's a particular area or piece of furniture that is bothering you, begin there. If not, always begin with your desk and move outward.

Step 2: Eliminate Stress by Removing Energy Drainers

Whether your office space is the CEO's corner suite, a cubicle, or the spare bedroom, after uncluttering, your next step is to remove energy-drainers. Remove anything blocking the balanced flow of energy. Clutter and energy-drainers are the two areas where stress begins and productivity stops. The more clutter and energy-drainers you have, the less efficient and productive you can be, which ultimately leads to more stress. Therefore, remove anything that distracts you, prevents you from focusing, or creates more stress.

Energy-drainers can be anything from too many family photos to stacks of files, magazines, and paperwork. Eliminate them, organize them, or file them. An energy-drainer can also be that dying plant in the corner taking up room, as well as the improper placement of functional items like the telephone, the computer monitor in relation to the keyboard, notebooks, pens, and so on. Remove the dead plant and move the functional equipment to a more convenient location.

Carefully look around your office for anything that leads you to focus your energy on past negative events. Every time you look to the past, you reinforce that negative energy. Eventually, as many of us know, the past can rule your life. Remove any items from your office and your filing cabinets that reinforce negative energy and thinking. Once those items are gone, you'll be better able to focus on the future, and you'll feel uplifted and motivated. The more positive energy you can bring into your life, the better you'll be able to deal with the negatives that occasionally pop up.

Lower your stress and replace it with success by eliminating clutter and arranging your office and desk space to maximize efficiency and productivity. If that means getting new filing cabinets or eliminating everything on the top of your desk, take time *now* to make those improvements.

The final energy-drainer that you may or may not be able to control in your office space is the color of the walls surrounding you. As we've discussed in other applications, wall color can create supportive, motivating energy or can drain your energy. Usually, the best colors for office walls are white or a light green. White is a high-energy yang color that supports productivity, while light green promotes new business and income growth. A soft green is especially good in offices that deal with a lot of high tech or anxious customers, clients, or patients.

Sometimes, of course, the wall color choice is not up to you. In that case, energize your space with additional white or green accessories. If you have a home office or do have the ability to change the color of your office, you could also add an earth-tone color, because it stimulates relationships with self and others, along with providing you grounding, so your activities will be more productive.

Once you've removed the energy-drainers and maximized your office for efficiency, it's time to shift the energy to make it positive and supportive.

Step 3: Create Supportive, Productive Energy

Now that you've completed Steps 1 and 2, it's time to create new positive energy that will support your productivity and prosperity objectives. Maintaining motivation, focus, and productivity are the key factors when evaluating whether the office is properly set up and energized.

Properly setting up and energizing your space will make a noticeable improved difference in your productivity…and others will notice. Through this process, you'll positively shift the energy for the entire area where you work, which, in turn, will help others plus the company you work for.

- Locate your desk so you either face the door or entrance area of your office or workspace, or always have the entrance in peripheral view. This puts you in a position of power, safety, and focus. (See Office Layout diagram.)
- If you can't move your desk into this preferred position, place a mirror on your desk so you can always view someone approaching you from behind. If possible, never sit with your back to the door; this is very distracting, unnerving, and prevents clarity and focus. (See Cubicle Layout diagram.)
- Make sure your computer keyboard and monitor are lined up for efficient use. This rule applies to all equipment.
- Place your telephone in a location that's easily accessible and leave ample space for writing and taking notes. Do not place it behind you as you will waste time and energy turning around to answer it.
- Keep notepads, pens, and a calendar adjacent to the telephone to maximize productivity.

From Clutter and Stress to Workplace Success

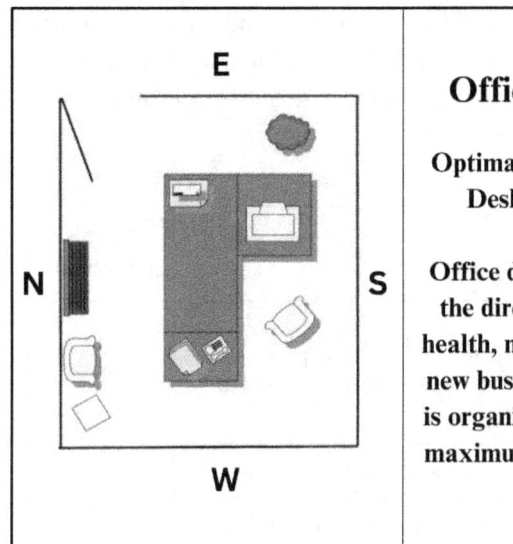

Office Layout

Optimal Placement of Desk and Chair

Office door faces east, the direction of good health, new growth, and new business. The desk is organized to promote maximum productivity.

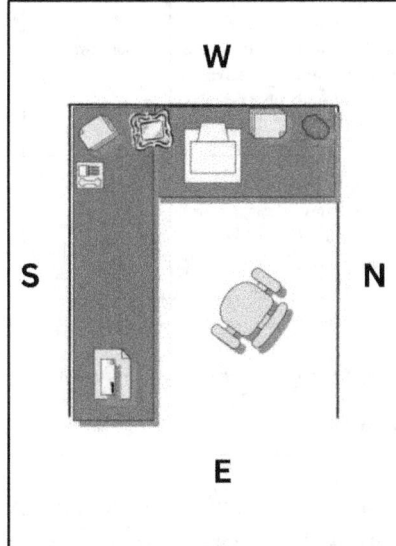

Cubicle Layout

Least Productive Placement of Chair

To create better energy and focus place a mirror on the desk so you have a view of anyone walking up behind you.

Cubicle faces west to support creativity.

Use your Shape of Life Map by laying it over your office floor plan and aligning the directions. Then take positive steps to energize the wealth, good luck, relationships, and helpful-people areas of your office.

To Enhance	Add	In This Direction
Wealth and Growth	A healthy, upward-reaching plant, a picture of trees, flowers blooming, or the color green	East
Luck and Good Fortune	Something bright red or triangular and upward-pointing like mountains or pyramids, the color red in a picture, or a mostly red vase	South
Relationships	Something symbolizing a happy and respectful relationship, such as a bouquet of flowers or a grouping of animals (such as giraffes in multiple sizes) or something made from terra cotta clay or the color terra cotta; perfect area for family photos and pictures showing great client relationships	Southwest
Helpful People	Something silver like a trophy or bowl, a team-effort picture, a teamwork poster, or picture of people who have helped you, framed in silver	Northwest
Career and Knowledge	Books, framed certifications, trade journals, or training manuals that will aid growth and advancement; if studying to pass a licensing exam, use relevant books, CDs, and exam information	Northeast

If your work space is a cubicle, make these energy enhancements on your cubicle walls or small areas on your desk.

Before you energize the top of your desk, make sure you have no clutter on it, especially by your telephone or computer. Uncluttering your desk will make a major difference in your productivity and ability to focus, concentrate, and be in control. Find more efficient ways to organize your active projects, either on top of your desk or in it. Keep current materials nearby and place the others into a holding area or vertical filing system.

If your desk is large enough, use your Shape of Life Map to locate and energize the east or southeast portion of it with a healthy plant or a wooden container with seven U.S. dollar coins inside to further energize wealth or income. Also, put something silver in the northwest area (a silver pen set, a silver world globe, or a silver business card holder would work nicely) to further energize your helpful-people area.

As you take a second look around your office and your desk, remember that clutter also includes all those cute things on the desk or walls, including pictures of family, children, or grandchildren. All those eyes are very distracting and not conducive to staying focused and being productive. Keep them to a minimum and place them in the southwest relationships corner of your desk or the southwest area of your office. If they won't fit, keep only the newest or most important one or two and take the rest home.

Define Success to Increase Clarity

What's your definition of "success"? Is it a promotion, more income, greater status within the company? You need to be specific about your goals. Otherwise, as the Cheshire Cat in *Alice in Wonderland* said, "If you don't know where you're going, how will you know when you get there?"

State your goals clearly and be specific. A good sample of a goal statement is: "I want to increase my income by 40%. In order to do that, I need the full cooperation of my office team so I can concentrate on bringing in new business and expanding existing business." When you have a well-defined goal, you can effectively use Feng Shui techniques to help focus the positive energy needed to achieve it.

Another example of a clear goal is: "By the end of two years, I want a promotion to sales manager. Therefore, I am going to focus my attention on improving relationships with clients so I can increase the number of clients and improve client retention. This will also help me increase the income I generate, making me stand out to the executive team."

By clarifying your definition of success or your goals, you will reduce your stress and improve your focus and productivity. You *will* achieve higher levels of prosperity and success!

Improving the flow of positive energy in your office doesn't need to cost anything but your time, a bit of determination, and some organizational skills. Remove the stagnant energy created by clutter and energy-drainers and enjoy the positive changes in your life, both at work and at home. Remember, though, to follow these steps in the order presented. If you focus energy on the cluttered areas before removing the clutter, the obstacles in your life will become worse, not better. And you'd be even further away from reaching your goal of more prosperity and success.

Feng Shui Can Help You on Your Journey to Success

Feng Shui is a simple and effective tool to use on your journey to success. It's all about eliminating the negative and stagnant energy that creates stress and anxiety and using positive energy to bring about the desired results—success!

Energizing an office and your life for success is no different than energizing a home for abundance or health. You always start by removing the clutter. Then you systematically energize various areas, depending on your goals and objectives, using your Shape of Life Map. The side benefit to energizing your office is that it has a wonderful ripple effect. You've tossed the pebble of new positive energy into the office and the ripples will reach out to all those who work in the office, the people with whom they interact, and their family members at home. Positive energy is contagious, just like a smile. The more positive energy you surround yourself with, the more it returns to you.

Create your own positive-energy action plan today. Remove the clutter and the energy drainers so you can shift the energy to supportive and positive. By doing so, you will change your world into an energized, stress-free, productive environment, with a minimum amount of time and effort.

Chapter 11

How to Thrive—Not Just Survive—the Holidays

Do you love the holidays? Or do you dread their arrival because of all the chaos, money, and time demands? Do you want to celebrate but can't seem to get your act together to make it happen? Even worse, do you live in an area where you feel that you can't celebrate as you wish for political or cultural reasons?

Celebrate the intent of *your* holidays. Stand firm in *your* beliefs and convictions and celebrate *your* holidays. When you do, those celebrations will provide you much positive energy that you can store and draw on all year long.

When there's an opportunity to celebrate a special holiday in your world, celebrate it with great enthusiasm. Savor the moments you share with family, friends, neighbors, and even strangers you run into at the grocery store or the mall parking lot. Decorate your home and celebrate with all your heart. Doing so creates great positive energy.

Enjoy the Holidays More

We often think the holidays are the perfect time to spend with family and friends in an idyllic setting. Whether you are celebrating Christmas, Independence Day, Kwanza, or Chinese New Year, are your holidays always picture-perfect? Or are there times when your turkey is overcooked and your shopping left until the last minute? Do you feel like you have constant reminders everywhere you look of how much you have left to do and how little time is available in which to do it?

Rest assured that you are not alone! All your expectations, in addition to the expectations of family members and friends, are difficult, if not impossible, to live up to, resulting in much stress. Holiday demands can strain relationships beyond recoverability. Is this year going to be different for you and your family? Have you promised yourself that you will not overcommit, overdo, overbuy, and overeat?

You can enjoy the holidays more this year. Start by promising yourself that your relationships with your family members and friends are much more important than setting the perfect table or baking one more batch of cookies.

The gift of shared time is truly priceless. Yes, you do want every holiday to be memorable. But there's a huge difference between being memorable and being enjoyed by all. Keeping stress levels down, and uplifting your personal energy with your relationships, begins with you. Make a commitment to yourself to have a simpler, more engaging holiday season so you can enjoy every precious moment you have together with your loved ones. As a reminder, place a red candle in a safe container in the south area of your living/family room (locate that area with your Shape of Life Map) and surround it with symbols of why you celebrate the holidays. Burn that candle at least one hour every night to help you focus on the promise you made to yourself. Then, watch your relationships glow and grow during the holidays.

The holidays are often extremely busy, with people and children of all ages wanting a piece of your time and energy. Instead of the usual "too much to do, too little time to do it in," take a more balanced approach to celebrating. Restore or create some new family holiday traditions. Rekindle relationships with family members and revitalize old friendships. Take a "casual elegance" approach to your celebrating.

Deliberately spend time with your family by watching favorite holiday movies with the fireplace burning or candles glowing, and do this well in advance of the upcoming holiday. Have children participate in decorating your home. Does it really matter if the tree is bottom heavy with decorations, since little ones can only reach the first three feet of the tree? Will anyone care if the candles in the menorah are slightly crooked?

Have everyone participate in the baking process. Use the strong hands of adults for mixing and kneading and little fingers for sprinkling the colored sugar sparkles on the top of the frosted cookies. Have the seniors participate by taste-testing, a favorite pastime for all ages.

All the festive decorations of this season, the colorful bright lights, the gifts, and the wonderful foods are great personal energy-builders that help carry you through what might be an otherwise difficult time ahead.

The holiday colors contain great positive energy and fit nicely into the Feng Shui Five Element Cycle. Green represents the element wood, which energizes good health and wealth. Red represents the fire element, which provides great fame and good luck. Blue, associated with both Hanukkah and

Christmas, embodies career and the spiritual energy of the element water. Hanukkah's silver, and the silver and gold ornaments on a Christmas tree, represent the element of metal, which encompasses everything from creativity and children to travel and helpful people. Many of the ornaments of the season are made of blown glass or fired ceramics, making them a great symbol of the element earth, which influences positive relationships and a grounded lifestyle. The bright lights further energize all who celebrate.

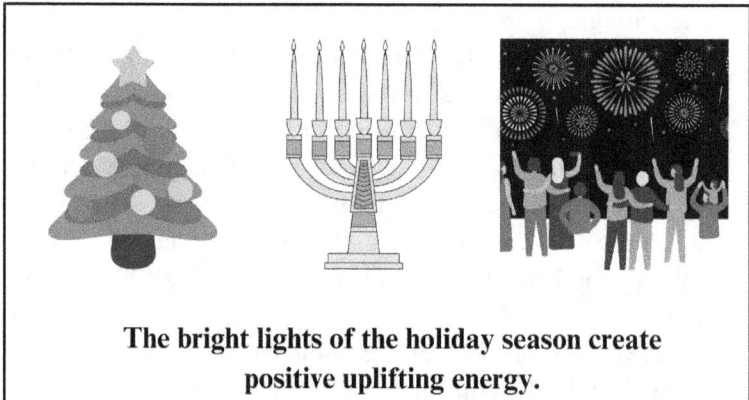

The bright lights of the holiday season create positive uplifting energy.

Create Positive Energy by Being Thankful

If you live in country that celebrates a Thanksgiving holiday, reflect on what that day means to you. Does Thanksgiving mean something special to you? Is it one of those holidays you celebrate but aren't sure why? Or do you look forward to Thanksgiving because it means great food and family and friends gathered around your table?

Thanksgiving has come to mean many things. But I believe most people use it as a time to reflect and be grateful for what they have in life. It's a holiday to appreciate family and friends, to share time with others, and to enjoy that wonderful positive energy such gatherings generate. Not only is your body nourished with the abundance of good food and drink, but your soul is nourished as well because of your intent for celebrating this specific holiday—that of showing gratitude.

Even though we celebrate this holiday only once a year, the showing of gratitude gives us uplifting energy we can store for later. It gives us hope for the future and appreciation for what we have. Gratitude energy is the type of energy that we all need to nurture ourselves with—*all year long*—so that we can benefit from its peace and hopefulness. There are several Feng Shui tools you can use to maintain this wonderful energy year-round.

- Create a small area on your kitchen counter or table where you can place a bowl of fresh fruit all year long. It doesn't have to be big and it can be any type of fruit. But it should always be full and items replaced when eaten. Fruit is the symbol of abundance and will remind you of the gratitude from Thanksgivings past and those yet to come. If you absolutely cannot use fresh fruit, then use the best looking, brightest colored faux fruit you can find. Be sure to keep the faux fruit clean and well dusted at all times.
- Find something symbolic of Thanksgiving that you can keep on display all year in the south area of your living room. It should remind you of your gratitude for good fortune or luck and for all that you have, including family, friends, health, and prosperity. It can be as simple as a picture of you and your family or friends gathered at a happy celebration, or a picture of praying hands. It can be large or small; size doesn't matter as long as you receive

the energy of abundance and gratitude from it every time you look at it.

- In the southwest area of your living room, place a beautiful earth-tone container filled with a bouquet of flowers in colors you love and in a variety of sizes and shapes. This special bouquet will constantly remind you of your abundance of family members and/or friends and your gratitude for times shared, whether in the present, the past, or yet to come. Use live flowers if you're diligent about replacing them weekly. Otherwise, use a lovely collection of silk flowers.

The energy of gratitude for things present, past, and future carries with it one of the greatest of energies—peace within. Everyone starts their journey in life with joy, hope, and peace built in, but we must remember to re-energize each area through simple thoughts like being thankful.

A gratitude attitude provides abundant peace within.

Energize Now to Ensure a Joyful Holiday Season

Whether you live in snow country or where palm trees wave year-round, the holidays are filled with the most wonderfully positive energy of the year. If you'd like to create a memorable, joyous holiday season, always begin well in advance. Eliminate negative-energy producers that make you feel overwhelmed and distract you from all the reasons you celebrate the holidays.

Unclutter First

Begin in *early fall* with the most common negative or stagnant energy distractions—clutter. Every place you have "stuff" or clutter stashed, stagnant energy collects…and chaos sets in. The less clutter you have, the more positive energy you have in your surroundings. You'll also have more time to do those things that are important, such as plan a memorable holiday season you can thoroughly enjoy with family and friends. If something is no longer functional or does not provide you positive energy…*get rid of it.*

Energize Next

The holidays are when we all try to put aside the negative energy in our lives and allow the wonderful positive energy we call joy, peace, love and hope into our homes, offices, and personal environment. While basking in the glow of this wonderful time of year, take note of what creates so much positive energy. What makes this season so enjoyable is that it satiates all five of our senses, while providing us hope for peace and joy. No other time of year touches our hearts in this way or nurtures us so much.

Listen

In order to preserve this positive holiday energy all year long, listen carefully to the sounds of the season. Notice the hustle of shoppers scurrying with bags of gifts and food or the rustle of wrapping paper. Add to that the ringing of chimes, the sound of the doorbell when special guests arrive, and the Christmas music that appears the day after Thanksgiving. Music is one of this holiday's major positive energizers. We hear these beautiful, inspirational, and fun holiday songs only during this time, as most people choose not to play this music year-round. However, there are thousands of other fun, inspirational, and wonderful pieces of music that carry the same uplifting energy of the holiday music no matter what holidays you celebrate. Enjoy the energy created by the sounds of the season all year.

Feel

Whether you think "feel" means the act of touching something or a sensation you experience on the inside doesn't matter. Either works for creating lots of positive energy. Touching and hanging family heirloom ornaments, as well as those newly purchased, provides deep-rooted positive energy. Be sure to also include all those hugs, smiles, and good wishes you receive.

Taste

Food, food, and more food shows up during the holidays, in the form of hors d'oeuvres, pastries, mulled wines, and tons of baked goods. Each morsel is more delectable than the previous. These sumptuous, mouthwatering foods contribute to the wonderful holiday energy we so cherish.

Smell

Right along with the enjoyable foods come the fragrances of the baked goods, the scented burning candles, the chestnuts roasting, and the pine boughs. To many of us, there's no finer smell than that of a freshly cut pine tree when it enters our home. It brings with it the fresh smell of the great outdoors, no matter what part of the country you live in.

See

The sights of the season are everywhere—in colorful lights, symbols, clothing, and food. For some, the sights include a peaceful layer of new fallen snow, while for others it's palm trees waving covered with millions of little white lights. Each of these carries wonderful positive-energy visions of the season. The indoor decorations are displayed with great care, along with lots of lights and candles burning brightly. Candles are filled with a warm, glowing positive energy, along with the twinkling decorations and lights that further set the scene for the holidays. Don't limit your candles' glow to the holidays. Let them burn brightly throughout the year for uplifting, radiating energy.

The holiday season is truly filled with hope, joy, peace, and love. Enjoy every minute of it. And absorb its wonderful, uplifting energy into your heart and soul. Use it as an example of the great positive energy that can surround you throughout the year.

Try some of the ideas in the stress-reducing guide below to increase calm and joy during the holidays.

Holiday Stress-Reducing Guide

- Do the most important thing on your "Holiday To-Do List" first—not the easiest or fastest one to complete but rather the one that will make your celebration perfect.
- Do only what must be done during the last couple of weeks before Christmas, Hanukkah, New Year's Eve, or the holiday you are celebrating. Anything that can wait and does not contribute to the organization and calm of a joyful celebration must be put on hold.
- Wear something comfortable and blue if you feel particularly stressed and find yourself living in chaos. In fact, dress from head to toe in blue. It is a very calming color and will help relieve some of that stress you are experiencing.
- Do fun things while gift wrapping. Steep some mulled cider on the stove and take an occasional sip along with a

bite of freshly baked holiday cookies. While wrapping presents, you can also watch one of the wonderful new or old Christmas movies that are sure to bring a smile to your face.

- Remember to buy yourself a wonderful gift while out shopping. It is good energy for you to treat yourself, along with everyone else on your list.

New Year's Resolutions That Matter

Do you routinely make New Year's resolutions? Will they improve your energy in the new year? And are they important enough that you stick to them?

Most people have great intentions and make many wonderful New Year's resolutions. But by January 20, at least half of those resolutions are long forgotten. What is on your resolution list? The following three resolutions are a "must" for a better year ahead.

1. **Simplify.** Whether you're young or old, male or female, you need to simplify your life and surroundings. Simplify your world by getting rid of all of the "stuff" that's no longer relevant to your life. Doing so will allow positive new energy to enter your home and your life in the new year. If something you are getting rid of is usable, pass it along to someone who needs it. You'll receive additional positive energy simply by making someone else happy. Once you've simplified your world, sit back and enjoy the fresh new energy meandering through. Bask in it...and do not fill up any newfound empty space with more stuff! Until you make room for it, new fresh energy cannot find its way into your home and your personal life, bringing with it opportunities, prosperity, and abundance.

2. **Focus your energy.** Look at all the activities you participate in. Do these things energize you or nurture you in some way? Helping others can be energizing if you don't overdo it. However, some activities you participate in could be energy-drainers. Evaluate every organization you belong to or every event you support with your time and/or money. Then decide to focus most of your energy on only those things you really love...and they will energize you as much as you energize them.
3. **Examine your thinking.** Are you telling yourself that you're a great person and can do anything you put your mind to? Or are you constantly putting yourself down and creating negative energy within? Unfortunately, it's easy to put yourself down and deplete your much-needed energy. Be determined to lift yourself up with encouraging, success-oriented thinking, so you can build good, positive energy within.

Simplifying your life is the quickest way to energize yourself and to improve the year ahead. Make your list, include the above suggestions, and then *do it*. You'll be pleasantly surprised at how good you feel about yourself after accomplishing even one of your resolutions.

I resolve to ...

- **Simplify my life**
- **Focus my energy on things I love**
- **Use encouraging, success-oriented thinking**

Thrive on Holiday Energy—All Year Long

It doesn't matter if you celebrate Christmas, Hanukah, New Year's, or any other holiday. The winter holiday season is filled with positive energy. Observe this wonderful energy, bask in its glow, and take advantage of it. Then *make it last all year long*!

Whether you're still in the middle of your celebrations or enjoying fond memories of that wonderful time months later, take note of what creates so much positive energy during the holidays. Remember, what makes this season so enjoyable is that it satiates all your senses while providing you hope, peace, and joy.

Maintain a very full memory bank of all the positive holiday energy you've experienced. Simply observe it and save it in your memories to draw upon when life is more challenging. Use this abundance of positive energy now to help you thrive, not just survive, the holidays. Then use it all year long as well.

You can use Feng Shui principles and apply them to any celebratory event in your life. You've learned many ways to create balance and harmony in your personal world, whether it's the holidays, an upcoming wedding, or major travel plans. Just follow the principles of Feng Shui set out at the beginning of this book and apply the ideas set out in the Holiday Stress-Reducing Guide to your event. Do the most important things first, and do only those things that must be done before your event. Be sure to wear comfortable clothing, do some fun things along the way, and energize yourself with a treat. It works for all kinds of events.

Chapter 12

Conclusion: Stepping Stones

While Feng Shui is a vast and sometimes confusing subject, it can be simplified so you can use it every day to take control of and create a better, more joy-filled life. This book is a user's manual, filled with practical advice and specific tools that can reduce stress, create calm, and increase prosperity and abundance.

In a stressful, anxious world filled with uncertainty, the information in this book provides the stepping-stones to low-cost, simple ways to feel more secure and in control of your personal environment. Additionally, each of these stepping-stones has guided you on a journey that leads you to "Feng Shui" your thinking. Once you bring your surroundings and your goals into alignment, the next step is to positively energize your thinking. The result is an unstoppable, calm, and in-control you.

Recipe for Positive Thinking

If you're still struggling with the "if only" or "it always happens to me" malady, read on. Is negative thinking still getting you down? Are you constantly telling yourself that nothing ever goes right? Has an argument, a mishap, or a bad experience with a neighbor, friend, or colleague got you down? Are these thoughts on auto-replay in your mind three months later? A year later? And do these constant thoughts make you feel increasingly anxious or depressed?

We all suffer from anxious moments, and we all feel down occasionally. But if these feelings are part of your daily routine, perhaps it's time to evaluate your surroundings and your thinking to determine if some additional positive energy will help. If you continue to focus on things that make you anxious and depressed, you'll continue to attract more negative-energy situations and thoughts that create even more anxiety and despair. What you focus on is what you get! What you have is what you have focused on up until now. What you think about *now* is what you create for your future.

Positive Thinking = Positive Results

When Norman Vincent Peale wrote his book *The Power of Positive Thinking* in 1952, he understood the impact of negative thoughts. He knew that if people focused their thoughts on positive things, they could change their lives for the better. This same principle is at work in Earl Nightingale's book, *The Strangest Secret,* written in 1956. And it's at the core of a book called *The Secret* by Rhonda Byrne in 2006. The good news is that you now have another tool, Feng Shui, that you can use to enhance your ability to stay positive instead of dropping back and focusing on the negatives.

As noted in earlier sections, in the world of Feng Shui, balance and harmony are the ultimate objectives, both in your surroundings and in your mind. However, even if you have perfect balance in your surroundings, if you are always thinking negative thoughts and focusing on the things that have gone wrong in your life, you'll have difficulty maintaining that balance and harmony. Accordingly, you'll continue to attract negative things, which snowball into even more things going wrong.

Positive Energy Shifts = Positive Thinking

To stop the constant mental replay of things that went wrong in your life, shift to positive energy in your *thoughts*. Here are a few easy-to-apply suggestions on how to create positive energy on the inside, so you can permanently push the "stop" button on negative thinking and create the kind of life that goes your way more often.

- Step into the light. Go outside where the sun is shining and take a walk. If you must stay indoors, open your curtains or turn on bright lights in your home. Invest in a torchiere lamp that shoots light upward for your favorite room. Light automatically raises your energy levels and thoughts.
- Spend time in brightly colored rooms when you're feeling down. Purchase brightly-colored accent pillows or a bright throw for the sofa to cheer up your favorite room. It will also cheer *you* up. If you're feeling anxious, spend time in a room that's painted calming colors like blue and green. You will respond positively to the calming energy of these colors.

- Wear light or bright colored clothing—yellow and orange work great—when you feel despair setting in; these colors will lift your spirits. Wear calming soft blues and greens when feeling anxious. These colors can change your outlook on life quickly from negative to positive.
- Create a Gratitude Journal. Write down at least five things you are thankful for every day. If you can't think of anything, start with things like having a roof over your head or food on the table, or having the ability to walk from your bedroom to the kitchen. Anything will do until you get the hang of it. The more grateful you are for everything in your life, the less time you have to feel sorry for yourself. You'll soon realize that a lot more things have gone your way than you thought.
- Play uplifting, nurturing music instead of listening to the six o'clock news. You have many music options today so choose wisely. The wrong choices can rob your spirit and create even more anxiety and depression. If you want to stir up your energy, play a few John Phillip Sousa marches. There is no way you can listen to them and remain in a negative thinking space. If you're anxious, play classical music like Mozart or peace-within music by artists like Steven Halpern. Music is the universal language. It can make the heart dance and the spirit soar, creating an abundance of positive energy.

Shift Energy to Create Positive Thinking

Go for a walk
Turn the lights on
Do creative journaling
Listen to uplifting music

These Feng-Shui-based suggestions can energize your world, guide you to positive thinking, and reduce stress, anxiety, and feelings of despair and depression. So often the solution is in your own backyard—in this case your own home plus your mind.

Some doubters underestimate the power of positive thinking but it's truly the ideal form of Feng Shui. Align your personal environment and your goals with your inner self and you'll create long-lasting inner peace and balance. When you replace the "if only" or "bad things always happen to me" thought process with positive energy, positive thinking is the result. And when you think positively, you take control of your outer and inner life.

What Does Your "Balance" Look Like?

Ultimately, the decision is yours when it comes to your concept of balance in your life and how you obtain it. The previous chapters provided you a series of stepping-stones in various areas of your life to achieve this balance. I guarantee that by applying this information, you *can* achieve balance and harmony and it will make a huge positive difference in your life. But you're the one in charge. I can only give you the information. You must apply the Feng Shui principles to make it happen.

If you are balancing being a working mother of three children, participating in school activities, and carving out time for yourself, uncluttering your surroundings and using Feng Shui principles will help get rid of the chaos and make your life run more smoothly.

If you're a CEO trying to balance your career, your health, and your personal relationships, incorporating Feng Shui principles will enable you to become more focused and productive, leaving you more time for those desired positive-energy relationships.

If you're overcommitted and have no time for *you*, you can find balance through uncluttering your life and applying the Feng Shui principles dealing with self-care.

If you're the high-tech type and have a problem connecting on a personal level with people, look closely at the relationships area of your home and workplace. Also, evaluate your thinking. You have to love yourself first to build the bridge to a long-lasting relationship.

What Are You Trying to Balance?

Being Overcommitted
Career, Family, and You
Time, Money, and Relationships
Connecting on a Personal Level

Remember, it costs very little money to make huge positive changes in your life, but it will require an investment in time and commitment on your part. Feng Shui lifestyle changes take desire, determination, and a deep commitment to self and creating a better life.

Your Personal Roadmap

Use the chapters in this book as an instructional manual to create your roadmap for eliminating chaos in your life and reaching your goals. Use the Shape of Life Map as a tool to help guide you to the answers that will work for you. This manual provides you basic information on how to shift from negative to positive energy in all areas of your life—relationships, health, luck, creativity, career, productivity, and even inner wisdom and spirituality.

Because each of us is different, the roadmap you create for yourself will not work for your spouse, friend, or neighbor. Your roadmap is individualized for you and will work only for you. In this case, one size does not fit all. However, the principles of Feng Shui, plus uncluttering your world and using the Shape of Life Map, work universally and equally well for everyone.

Use the various sections of this book as a positive energy guide that will provide you insight and direction when making purchases, redecorating, changing jobs, moving to a new home, and rebuilding old or creating new relationships. Carry this book with you when making household and clothing purchases to check the energy your purchases will provide you. Simply follow the directions on how to create your own personal roadmap and you'll succeed in creating a better, more productive, and more enjoyable life.

Does Feng Shui Really Matter?

In the grand scheme of things, does Feng Shui really matter? Will it really make a difference in your life? Is it a lifestyle you and your family should adopt? Is it a lifestyle your workplace or business should adopt?

Conclusion: Stepping Stones

The answer to these questions lies in another question. "Do you want to be in control of your life, your family relationships, and your workplace so you can enjoy a more prosperous and abundant life?" Perhaps even more important is to answer this question: "Do you want to look within and connect with your higher self, your Creator?" When you create a home and workspace environment that is clam, chaos free, quiet, and peaceful, you have opened the door to finding your eternal connection with God. When surrounded with silence and peace, you can hear that loving quiet voice within, the voice of your Creator. This is the ultimate connection for creating a better future.

After all, Feng Shui is about using positive energy in your personal environment and the workplace to take control of your life. It's about personal empowerment, *your personal self-empowerment,* and it's about a life where you can relieve stress and anxiety while creating balance and harmony in your surroundings and within yourself.

Feng Shui is an ancient philosophy or lifestyle that is just as effective today, in our multitasking, hardwired, stress-filled world, as it was 3,000 years ago. And the reason is simple—it works.

It works because you use a simple process in which everything is filled with either positive or negative energy. If you surround yourself with the positive-energy things, thoughts, and people, your life will improve. If you surround yourself with negative-energy things, thoughts, and people, your life cannot get better…and it may even get worse. Negative energy is stagnant energy. Stagnant energy prevents forward movement.

Is Positive Change on Your Calendar?

Making the case for using Feng Shui is simple. Its principles are results-oriented and thus provide you the tools to achieve your goals. These tools help you create balance in your life and in your personal environment by using color, shape, and sound. Feng Shui also provides you with a formula for the placement of household and workplace objects that can generate uplifting, supportive energy so you can remove stress and become calmer and more productive.

The same tools will help you transform your home into a peace-filled refuge—a sanctuary from a frantic outside world filled with visual, air, and noise pollution, cement cities, constant media bombardment, multitasking, and being in constant contact but never being connected.

Everything, *everything*, in your surroundings has energy—your clothes, the colors of your walls, the car you drive, the health club you frequent, and the people you hang out with. This is the same energy recorded in the famous Einstein formula $E=mc^2$. All these things provide you either uplifting energy or success-limiting energy.

But, if you wish to experience the dramatic and positive results Feng Shui can provide, you need to put these principles and tools into action. Make a commitment to creating a better life. Put it on your calendar and begin today.

The Result

Once you transform your life, your home, and your workspace through uncluttering your world and creating uplifting energy that's aligned with your goals and objectives, you'll create balance in your world and will allow positive energy to flow.

Conclusion: Stepping Stones

When your home and workplace feel balanced, with positive energy flowing, so does your mind and body.

The result of incorporating Feng Shui in your life will be a calmer, more focused, and more productive *you*. You will get more pleasure and joy out of life; hope, peace, and joy will abound. You will be better able to determine which things to keep and which to throw out, not only from your closets but also from your life.

You've also learned what you can control and what you can't. You're better able to live in the *now*, instead of worrying about past negative events or possible future events that may never happen. Ultimately, you've created an environment conducive to reconnecting to God and the universe, which is an incredible gift.

Use Feng Shui daily. It really does work. And it will help you take control of your life...not tomorrow, not next week...but right *now*.

You are special because you are you, and you deserve to have the best that life can offer. Just remember,

It's your life—take control of it!

Resources

Inspirational Music

Inner Peace Music by Steve Halpern
www.innerpeace.com

Information/Organizations

Feng Shui Society
377 Edgware Road
London VV2 1BT, UK
www.fengshuisociety.org.uk

Nine Star Astrology (Flying Star School)
by Jon Sandifer
P.O. Box 69 Teddington
Middlesex United Kingdom
jon@fengshui.co.uk

Shape of Life Map
Transparency available through
Pat Heydlauff
www.PatHeydlauff.com

About the Author

Pat Heydlauff, president of Energy Design, uses Feng Shui design principles to eliminate chaos and stress at home, in the office, and within oneself. More than a Feng Shui expert, Pat is a consultant and speaker who helps remove clutter and negativity while encouraging personal growth, improved relationships, and prosperity.

Through her columns, seminars, and presentations, she helps clients attain peace and a better quality of life. Pat's extensive knowledge of Feng Shui and design helps clients harmonize their homes and offices by creating environments with balance and a positive flow of energy.

Pat also works with professional business organizations to help them increase productivity and improve client relationships. She helps to develop Corporate Work/life Balance and Flow of Focus programs that result in increased visibility and reputation, which in turn, improve the bottom line.

Her artwork features a distinctive style, along with various imaginative media, to evoke emotions based on the science of Spiritual Energy. Pat's paintings, which range from spiritual to free-flow to mainstream, are displayed in galleries and public buildings throughout the U.S. and Europe, as well as the homes of celebrities.

For information on her consulting, speaking, and artwork, visit: www.PatHeydlauff.com.

www.ingramcontent.com/pod-product-compliance
Lightning Source LLC
Chambersburg PA
CBHW070425010526
44118CB00014B/1909